Growing
BEYOND ABUSE

A Workbook

for Survivors

of Sexual

Exploitation

or Childhood

Sexual Abuse

P9-CEC-538

Signe L. Nestingen, M. A.
Laurel Ruth Lewis

Omni Recovery, Inc.

Minneapolis, Minnesota

Growing Beyond Abuse.

Quotes reprinted by permission of Karen Casey, Dr. William Masters, Gary Schoener, Jeanette Milgrom and Melissa Roberts-Henry.

"Wheel of Options" reprinted by permission of authors, Schoener, Milgrom, Gonsiorek, Luepker and Conroe from *Psychotherapists' Sexual Involvement With Clients.* © 1989, Walk-In Counseling Center.

Excerpts from *The Angry Song* used by permission from Laurel Lewis. © 1990, Omni Recovery, Inc.

Workbook Design: Peggy Lauritsen Design Group

Editor: Louellyn Reiss Nestingen
Copy Editor: Barbara Barker
ISBN 0-9628703-0-7 (paper)

All correspondence
Omni Recovery, Inc.
P.O. Box 50033, Minneapolis, Minnesota 55403

Workshops and Lectures

Signe L. Nestingen and Laurel Lewis offer seminars, lectures and training workshops on topics related to sexual exploitation and childhood sexual abuse. If you would like to attend our lectures or workshops or invite us to speak in your area, please write to Omni Recovery, Inc.

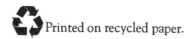Printed on recycled paper.

This is for Ed and Ruth, who have unconditionally supported and encouraged me in all my endeavors.

Signe

This workbook is dedicated to Walk-In Counseling Center, Peg Thompson, Ph.D., and the American Association of Marriage and Family Therapists for their professional integrity.

Laurel

Table of Contents

Introduction

Acknowledgments

Foreword

Definitions

How to Use This Workbook

Table of Contents

Introduction

Some years ago I was sexually exploited by a therapist/pastoral counselor. To survive this devastating experience I moved to Minnesota. For many months, after I moved, I was unable to trust anyone and unable to work. There are a number of people in Minnesota who are forerunners in helping those who have been sexually exploited. These experts, who understand the long lasting and devastating effects of sexual exploitation, were available to me. Working with these people I began my long and arduous healing journey.

I attended a group for survivors of sexual exploitation. Because of the incestuous dynamics of the abuse I also attended an incest therapy group. As I began to recover, I discovered a lack of information for survivors of sexual exploitation. I decided to record what I was learning in a series of daily meditations. At this point, Signe and I teamed up and wrote the meditations together. *Growing Beyond Abuse* evolved from these meditations.

As Signe and I worked on the meditations we were struck by the remarkable parallels in healing from childhood sexual abuse and sexual exploitation. We carefully incorporated what I was learning and Signe's expertise in using creative arts and journal writing with survivors of sexual abuse into *Growing Beyond Abuse*.

It is our sincere hope that this workbook will aid in your own healing from sexual abuse.

Laurel

~ ~ ~

Acknowledgements

There are numerous people who have helped and encouraged us in this endeavor. Jill Johnson, for her relentless consultation, deserves a special thank you. Thanks also go to Peggy Lauritsen, Karen Elliot and Louellyn Reiss Nestingen who were instrumental in providing design, editing and distribution ideas. Fred Meyer's facilitation in focus groups and product strategies was both timely and helpful.

For content guidance and direction we wish to thank Gary Schoener and Jeanette Milgrom of Walk-In Counseling Center. Their expertise was invaluable. A special thanks for both Nickey Larson and Melissa Roberts-Henry for their direct and thoughtful feedback.

We would like to thank Lucy, Maggie, M.J., Lynne, Becky, Sue, Loie, Marlene, Lynn, Clair and Ruth for their energy, laughter and diversity.

Thanks to Dr. William Masters, M.D. for his telephone consultation and support.

Sarah Fischer, Director of the Institute for Behavioral Medicine, Peter Dimmock, Rachel Lund, Jodi Dunlap, Susan Meyers and Deanne Halperin also deserve a big thank you for their contributions to us as we worked on this book.

A special thank you goes to Nancy T., Nancy Nurse and Connie for their emotional support.

The talent, creativity and energy of various members of The National Association of Women Business Owners has been critical to the completion of this project.

For the women and men who shared their stories and gave us quotes, we are touched and grateful. Thank you.

Foreword

Growing Beyond Abuse is a book whose time has come.

Not too many years ago, (recently enough for some of us to remember), rape "did not exist"; incest was a word people could not say out loud; and sexual exploitation by counselors, therapists and clergy was unheard of.

Now we know better. We now know that all these variations of the theme of sexual abuse do, indeed, exist. And we know they occur with considerable frequency and have devastating effects.

We recognize that the victim of sexual abuse (even if it occurred many years ago) needs to face the problem and work through it. In recent years we have arrived at the term "survivor", indicating a stage beyond being a victim. Growing Beyond Abuse speaks to yet another dimension.

In this book the authors take the survivor, as it were, by the hand, gently guiding the survivor through the garden of life during this new season. The reader is encouraged to take time to smell the flowers; pay attention to the rain, sun, wind and thunder; and to experience solid ground to stand on.

In doing so, the authors address the many aspects of the reader's life which may have been affected by the abuse: grief and loss, trust, sexuality and self-esteem to name a few. Growing Beyond Abuse speaks to the need for recovering, healing and growing in these various areas.

The authors' approach in Growing Beyond Abuse is sensitive without being sentimental. It has all the potential for being therapeutic without "therapizing" the reader. It is creative, poetic, and above all else: gentle and respectful. It invites the reader to engage in the process and the activities of healing and growing by participating in a series of readings and exercises, thus making the process concrete.

May this book help individuals grow beyond; to grow in strength and wisdom and insight; to reach out with compassion and generosity to themselves and others. And may this book serve as a gift, an aid and a tool to those who wish to grow beyond abuse, and also to those assisting others in the process.

Jeanette H. Milgrom
Director of Consultation and Training
Walk-In Counseling Center
Minneapolis, Minnesota

Sexual abuse occurs *without regard* for the exploited child, adolescent or adult. In a relationship which is sexually abusive, boundaries are violated and blurred; roles are reversed or confused; the needs of the dependent individual are ignored, or are secondary to those of the perpetrator; and mixed messages are sent to the dependent individual.

Relationships which are **sexually exploitative** occur when someone in a position of power, trust and authority promotes, encourages and establishes a sexualized relationship with a person in a position of dependency. These are *not consensual* relationships! The well-being of the dependent individual is disregarded. This includes, but is not limited to, physical, mental, emotional and spiritual well-being.

An **adult** can be **sexually exploited** by a professional. These professionals can include therapists, psychologists, doctors, psychiatrists, members of the clergy, professors, teachers, and mentors. Those who wear the cloak of professional authority and responsibility are expected to be ethical and trustworthy. Because of this, a person requesting professional services is especially vulnerable.

Childhood sexual abuse occurs when a child or adolescent is sexually exploited by someone in a position of trust and power. Perpetrators include, but are not limited to, teachers, baby-sitters, police officers, members of the clergy, scout troop leaders, coaches, neighbors or family friends. Childhood sexual abuse is **incestuous** if the offender is from the kinship circle.

Sexually abusive behavior can be physical, emotional or verbal. On a continuum, behavior which is sexually exploitative, ranges from nudity or genital exposure to violent penetration of the vaginal or anal area with a penis, fingers or objects. In a number of instances, role confusion and reversal are exploitative. Likewise, sexually intrusive jokes, comments and questions are exploitative.

~ ~ ~

How to Use this Workbook

This is a book to get involved with, write in, draw in, paint in, and spill coffee on. This book can be your friend, companion, aid, guide, teacher and helper. You might use this workbook alone and/or with other survivors. You might feel challenged, comforted, angered, excited and delighted. Our intention is that the workbook promote your healing. We believe it can serve as a convenient place to record your pain, sorrow, anger, growth, change and celebration as you grow beyond the abuse.

There are ten chapters or themes in *Growing Beyond Abuse*. Each chapter has two or more "Readings". Each reading is followed by four associated exercises that we call "Expressions".

Find a chapter or theme that appeals to you. Select a reading and plan to complete the four associated expressions following the reading. Because this workbook can elicit strong feelings we <u>encourage</u> you to do only one expression a day. You may, of course, spend more than one day working on an expression. You may decide you want to do two expressions in a day. (Turn the page to see an example).

Start any where you wish. Move from theme to theme. For example, if your focus is trust, work with a reading and the expressions in the "Trust" section of the book. When you are ready, move to another chapter, for example "Self Esteem" or "Denial", return to the "Trust" chapter if and when you are ready.

As you use this book you can spell, write or use any punctuation you wish. You can WRITE IN CAPITAL LETTERS IF YOU WANT TO, but you don't have to.

Draw, write, paint, sculpt with either or both hands. (Sometimes it is helpful to use your non-dominant hand as you work).

Work at your own pace. Put the book down and pick it up as you feel ready. If you and other survivors work together on this book, share <u>what</u> you are ready to share, <u>when</u> you are ready to share it.

We have used the term *sexual abuse* in many readings and writings. This is an umbrella term for *sexual exploitation, childhood sexual abuse* and *incest*.

In many exercises we have used the phrase <u>*create an image*</u>. This is shorthand for draw, paint, work with play-dough or clay, sculpt, color, make a collage or cut and paste various colors of paper to create any image you desire. When you find the phrase, <u>*create an image*</u>, please do what ever feels comfortable to you. Create drawings, poems, stories, songs or sculptures of your healing. If the images you create are too large for the workbook, you might choose to take photographs of your creations and put the photos in your book.

Need more room? Get a three ring notebook or add pages to your workbook. Use large pieces of paper to paint, draw or scribble on. Keep those papers in a special place for yourself.

If you have thoughts or fears about why you can *not* use a workbook that has exercises using drawing, painting, writing and other alternative forms of expression, try this exercise.

On a separate sheet of paper list the thoughts that inhibit your use of a workbook.
For example:
    I cannot write.
    My drawings are horrible.
When your list is complete, crumple or rip it up and throw it away.

On another sheet of paper write all the reasons you can use this workbook.
For example:
    I CAN write or draw if I want.
    This is my private book.
    I am important.
    I get to tell my story.
Keep this list in your workbook as new ideas about how and why you can use this book come to mind, add those to your list.

Wounds from sexual exploitation and childhood sexual abuse dig deep into the psyche. Recovery is more than physical, mental and emotional. The soul must also be healed. Because of this we have added a spiritual expression to do with each reading. These expressions can provide an opportunity to reach inside and connect with that *something greater* in the universe. This *something greater* may be making friends, connections with the earth, a relationship with a Supreme Being or a recognition that there is a bond between peoples.

There are times when we have used the words *something greater than myself* to represent a Supreme Being, God or Higher Power. Our hope was to find an inclusive term that works in most spiritual traditions. Please feel free to use any name you wish for that which you call God or Higher Power. Ideas might be Higher Self, Goddess, Spirit, Higher Spirit, Universal Power, Great Spirit or Creator.

The next three pages are a demonstration. A "Reading" and the four associated exercises or "Expressions" are completed. The theme is Anger.

Below is the Reading *Changing My Views About Anger*. This reading can be used as a meditation or thought for an hour, a day or a week before doing the associated exercises.

---

5 Anger

Changing My Views About Anger

My family had rules about anger.
  Lots of rules.
    ~ Some of the rules were spoken.
    ~ Some of the rules were not spoken.

Some of those rules were:
    ~ Do not get angry, get even.
    ~ Children do not get angry.
    ~ Anger is a bad thing, do not be angry.
    ~ Do not get angry with family members.
    ~ Getting mad means getting punished.
    ~ When someone gets mad, someone gets hurt.

Sometimes, in the past, anger and rage were violently expressed.
Sometimes, in the past, anger and rage were sexually expressed.

I have a deep rage about being abused.
Sometimes it feels very powerful. Too powerful to give voice to.
I am frightened, sometimes, by my rage.
    ~ I hold my rage in my body.
    ~ I hold my rage in my mind.
    ~ I hold my rage in my heart.
    ~ I do not speak or express my rage.

I want to move that anger to constructive channels.
I do not want to be a container of anger any longer.
I want to be free of the oppressive weight of my rage.
I want my anger to free me.
I want the productive energy of my anger to heal me.

reading

73

On the right is a completed example of *Changing My Views About Anger - Expression 1.* The exercise includes written responses to the questions asked.

In *Changing My Views about Anger - Expression 2,* a resource list to use when angry feelings or destructive thoughts arise is displayed. (Note: The names and phone numbers with x's were created for this example.)

How to Use this Workbook

A combination of drawing and writing is used in *Changing My View About Anger - Expression 3*. The actual drawing was made with different colors of crayon.

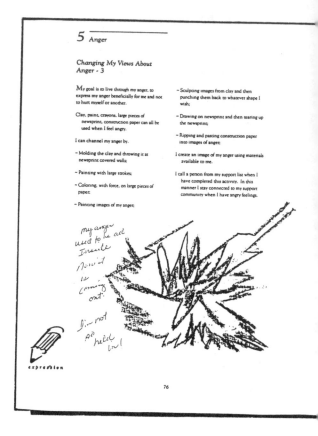

The last exercise is named *Changing My Views About Anger - Spiritual Expression**. A combination of drawing and writing is used once again.

*Some of the Spiritual Expressions are focused on taking care of the Earth.

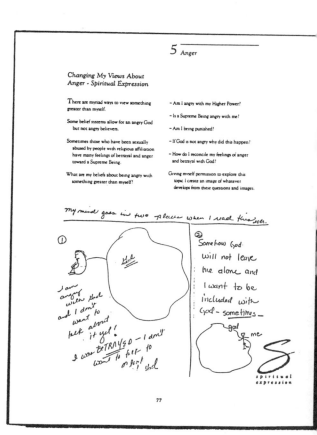

Denial

> "It seems like every time I go deeper, I hit another level of denial. I hang on to the fact that I have been there before and that I came to know truth."
>
> *Survivor*

1

1 Denial

Moving Through Denial

I was devastated by the sexual abuse.
Wanting to retreat and deny my memories, I
ask myself, did I make this up?

Did this really happen? Did this person I
trusted really abuse me?
   I want to protect myself.
   I have such pain.
   I want to wrap the fog of denial
   around me.
   I want to pretend my daily life was
   not effected.

Denial
   ~ kept me safe,
   ~ protected me,
   ~ held me close in a silent circle.
With fog swirling in my mind,
I dared not make changes.

Healing, I am learning
   ~ I can be safe.
   ~ I can protect myself.
   ~ I can find healthy ways to be safe
     without denial.
   ~ I can move through the pain the
     memories bring.
   ~ I can accept my memories.

reading

2

Moving Through Denial - 1

I am not alone,
though denial keeps me isolated.
I can reeducate myself and decrease my
shame and isolation.

Abuse is a local, national and international
phenomena.

Through my research I learn about others
who have been abused, have survived and
grown beyond abuse to live full lives.

I may want to know about these people.

When I am ready,

~ I may want to reach out and join
organizations that work to prevent abuse.

~ I may want to meet others who are healing.

Sometimes involving myself decreases my
denial.

To create a resource file, I list people and
places from which I can receive
information, education and support. I call
a friend, or a local helpline for ideas.

Today, on this page, I start to create my
resource file.

expression

1 Denial

Moving Through Denial - 2

My need for denial diminishes as I heal.

I ask myself how my daily life is effected by the sexual abuse?

~ Did I learn to be silent?

~ Did I learn that I am not important?

~When I want a connection with something greater than myself do I believe that NO ONE IS THERE?

~ Do I drink too much? Eat too much?

~ Am I afraid of the dark?

~ Am I afraid of men? Women?

~ Am I afraid to talk about my family? The abuser?

~ Do I resist change in my life?

How has my life been affected by the abuse? I answer this question by creating an image.

or -

I respond to one or more of these questions.

expression

Moving Through Denial - 3

How do I experience denial in my daily life?

~ Am I unwilling to listen to my body?

~ Do I pretend that I do not have feelings related to the abuse?

~ Do I ignore fragments of memories?

~ Do I keep anger locked inside because I should not be angry?

~ Do I drink, eat or play excessively to try to deny feelings?

~ Do I still need denial in my life? Why? Does it protect me?

~ Does denial keep me safe from pain I am not yet ready to feel?

In my journal I respond to one or more of these questions.

or -

I write about how I experience denial.

expression

1 Denial

Moving Through Denial - Spiritual Expression

Listening to others tell their story helps in many ways. It decreases my tendency to deny my pain and reminds me I am not alone.

Today I want to listen to someone else. I want to give my attention to someone else's need. I want to hear their story.

As I listen I hear echoes of my own story and I contribute to the storyteller's healing.

How do I feel when I really listen to another survivor's story?

What happens inside of me?

spiritual
expression

1 Denial

Growing Beyond Denial

When the abuse occurred I tried to protect
myself from the overwhelming stimulation.

I trained myself not to think, not to feel.
I learned
~ not to be vulnerable,
~ to stay all closed up,
~ to protect myself.

I learned
~ to ignore certain signals,
~ not to respond when the little voice
  said, "this isn't right",
~ to forget what happened.
~ not to dig too deeply into my mind
  because I might remember things I
  wanted to forget.
~ not to hope.

Now I want to
~ open my mind,
~ access buried information,
~ reclaim my memories,
~ remember what I worked so hard to
  forget.

Now I want to
~ listen to myself.
~ listen to the small, still voice.
~ learn to trust myself.
~ learn to be vulnerable and protect
  myself.
~ hope.

r e a d i n g

1 Denial

Growing Beyond Denial - 1

It may seem silly to learn to be vulnerable. I was vulnerable and I got hurt. I do not really want to be vulnerable, it does not seem safe.

As I heal I am learning that

~ I feel vulnerable,

~ I can protect myself when I feel vulnerable.

~ I can be vulnerable with safe people.

Today I list ways I protect myself when I feel vulnerable.

Some ways are:
I do not walk alone late at night or other unsafe times.

I ask others when I think something may not be correct.

I say NO to inappropriate touch.

I say NO to touch I do not like or want.

I say NO to involvement in situations I do not like.

Learning how I can protect myself while I feel vulnerable empowers me.

It is part of the reclamation of myself.

expression

Growing Beyond Denial - 2

As I learn more about sexual abuse I discover that disconnecting my feelings from my body was a coping skill.

Unfortunately, this means

~ that I may not listen to my body signals,

~ that I may not be able to listen to my body signals,

~ that I may not be aware of what my body is telling me.

Today

~ I want to start to connect with my body's knowledge.

~ I pay attention to my body as I experience feelings.

At the close of my day I jot down how my body felt as emotions arose.

expression

1 Denial

Growing Beyond Denial - 3

I needed to protect and shield myself while the abuse was occurring. Sometimes I blocked thoughts, feelings and ideas out of my mind, sometimes I shut down, sometimes I was silent or ate too much.

How did I shield myself while the abuse was occurring?

~ was I silent?

~ did I divert my mind? think about other things?

~ did I forget? care take?

~ did I think the abuse was love?

~ did I overeat? sleep? numb out?

~ did I suppress any doubts I had that this was not o.k.?

~ did I think that the perpetrator knew what was best for me?

~ did I deny what was happening or how bad I really felt?

Using the list as a guide, I write about the ways I shielded myself during the abuse.

or -

I create an image of the feelings and images that surface as I read through these questions.

expression

Growing Beyond Denial -
Spiritual Expression

Hope!

Hope was the last thing let out of Pandora's
   Box. All the evils of the world escaped
   and Hope was left locked inside the chest.
   Finally Hope was free.

Starting to heal is like that.
   Finally, there is hope.

What does it mean to hope?

What is it like for me to feel hope?

Can I believe that I deserve to hope
   for a life that is
      safe?
      whole?
      loving?

In the hour of time I take for myself, I
   respond to these questions and write about
   hope.

or -

I may create an image of hope for myself.

S

*spiritual
expression*

Memories

2

2 Memories

Body Memories in Recovery

What is a body memory?

Sometimes
> ~ my memories are not thoughts or
> pictures.
> ~ my memories come in feelings in my
> body.
> ~ I remember the abuse in my body.

At first
> ~ I felt frightened and alone with my
> body memories.
> ~ I was overwhelmed.
> ~ I did not know what to do to help
> myself.

I am learning
> ~ to stay with the memories.
> ~ to call someone.
> ~ to talk about my body memories with
> my support group.
> ~ to feel better when I am reassured by
> others who have body memories.
> ~ to allow myself to heal.

Sharing strengthens my resolve to live
> through these physical reminders of the abuse.

reading

Body Memories in Recovery - 1

One way to help myself with body memories is to become more familiar with how I feel about my body.

I draw a picture of my body and I

~ color in the areas I like with one color.

~ color in the areas I dislike with another color.

I draw another picture of my body and I

~ color in the areas of my body that were assaulted.

Comparing the drawings I wonder

What do the drawings say to me?

or -

What would it be like to love my whole body?

expression

Body Memories In Recovery - 2

Sometimes I blame myself and my body for the abuse.

Today I

~ write down one or two negative thoughts about my body and the abuse.

~ rewrite the negative thoughts as affirmations for my body.

For example:

I say negative things about my body
~I am ugly.
~I hate my breasts.
~I hate my build.

Affirmation:

~I am learning I am attractive.

~I am learning that my body is okay including my breasts.

~I am learning to appreciate my build.

expression

Body Memories In Recovery - 3

I had no control over what happened to my body during the abuse. My body memories remind me of this.

Sometimes, it is difficult for me to remember I can make choices about my body.

On this page I will write one or more things I can do for my body that I like.

For example:

~Exercising

~Walking

~Breathing Deeply

~Taking a Warm Bath

~Talking to my Pet

expression

Body Memories In Recovery -
Spiritual Expression

*T*oday I

~ create an image of my body free of abuse
    memories.

or -

~ create an image of how my body looks as it
    heals.

or -

~ create an image of my healthy body.

When I have body memories I can use this
    image as a reminder that I can grow
    beyond abuse.

spiritual
expression

Easing The Stress Of Memories

As memories of sexual abuse return I feel more stress in my daily life.

Sometimes my memories return in elusive ways.
  ~ I am overwhelmed by the persistent reminders of the abuse.
  ~ I feel myself slipping into old compulsive habits.
  ~ I slip into isolation or passivity.

I know that during the abuse I did not have many options for dealing with the stress of the abuse.

As I heal I can
  ~ learn new skills, new ways to cope.
  ~ recognize stressful memories and defend myself against them.
  ~ start to reduce the stress of memories by getting connected with others who understand.

reading

2 Memories

Easing The Stress Of Memories - 1

I have choices.

I can learn different ways to cope with stressful memories.

Today I make a list of things to do when memories of being abused return.

For example:

~ Journal

~ Draw

~ Walk

~ Call a support person

When memories return I can refer to this list to help me decrease my stress.

expression

Easing The Stress Of Memories - 2

When my memories of the abuse return, I feel tension start to build.

Sometimes

~ I remain silent because I have a secret that shames me.

~ staying silent when memories return increases my stress.

Making a list of people I can tell my story to

~ keeps me focused on my recovery,

~ eases the stress I feel,

~ comforts me.

Today I write on this page the names and phone numbers of one or more persons I can talk with about my memories. This list can include the phone number for helplines in my area.

or -

I can write down what I would like to talk about with someone helpful and supportive.

expression

2 Memories

Easing The Stress Of Memories - 3

Laughter greatly reduces stress.

Laughter reminds me that even in the midst of painful memories there is joy somewhere in my life.

Laughter gives me a rest from my memories and is a part of healing.

Today I can

~ close my eyes and think of a time when I laughed and laughed.

~ remember what it feels like to laugh and let go.

~ allow myself to surrender to a moment of pure joy.

Today I write about laughter.

expression

Easing The Stress Of
Memories - Spiritual Expression

I am learning that I can enjoy parts of my life as I heal from the abuse.

I am learning that even in pain I can find joy in my life.

Today I imagine myself in a moment of enjoyment.

I make the image clearer by asking;
What am I doing?
Is anyone with me?
Are we laughing? Playing?

Today I create an image of a moment I enjoyed.

or -

I call and invite someone to share a time in the past we each enjoyed. I write down how I felt doing this exercise.

spiritual expression

2 Memories

Memories And Reassurance

It is difficult to believe in myself, to believe the memories that cascade through me.

These painful memories seem like nightmares that will not cease.

Often
~ I wish to deny what happened.
~ I feel sad and angry.

As memories surface, I am tempted to say to myself I made this up.
As I recover I learn to trust myself, to listen to myself.

As I listen I find my truth.
~ I start to live my truth and my story!
~ I begin to believe in myself!
~ I begin to speak my truth!

r e a d i n g

Memories and Reassurance - 1

When memories of abuse return I need

~Reassurance
~Comfort
~Validation

Today I create a *Reassurance List.*

A reassurance list has at least 2 ways that I know I am reassured, comforted and validated.

I can refer to my reassurance list whenever memories of the abuse return.

For example:

~ I take care of myself and am comforted when I call a support person as memories of the abuse return.

~ I feel reassured when my support group validates my experience by listening to me or sharing some of their stories.

expression

2 Memories

Memories And Reassurance - 2

Today I write down one memory of the abuse.

I write some of the reasons I cannot and do not want to believe the memories of the abuse.

or -

I write how I feel when I believe in myself and my memories of the abuse.

expression

Memories And Reassurance - 3

Sometimes memories tire me out physically. I need to take care of my body when I remember painful episodes.

~ I can run,
~ walk,
~ swim,
~ play racquetball,
~ find a support person to be with me.

When painful memories return there are ways to take care of my body. I list two or more ways I can take care of my body.

expression

2 Memories

Memories And Reassurance - Spiritual Expression

Quiet time for myself is reassuring.

Today I will find some time to be quiet with myself.

~ I may sit in silence and meditate.

or -

~ I may listen to soothing music while remaining silent.

or -

~ I may create an image while silent.

I seek the reassurance of my quiet mind. I write how I feel about taking time for myself.

spiritual expression

28

Trust

> "Since I never had anyone safe to rely on as a kid, I didn't trust anyone. Now, if someone doesn't feel right to me, I trust my own feelings. I trust myself to say no."
>
> *Survivor*

3

3 *Trust*

Rebuilding Trust

Sexual abuse by a family member or an
individual in a position of power demolishes
trust.

At times I wonder
- ~ why should I trust?
- ~ what could I possibly gain by trusting
  another?
- ~ can I ever trust anyone again?
- ~ can anyone trust me?
- ~ how might I feel in a trusting
  relationship?

As I free myself from the net of abuse I am
learning
- ~ about trust;
- ~ to trust myself,
- ~ to trust my own judgment,
- ~ to trust others who are helpful and
  healthy for me.

r e a d i n g

Rebuilding Trust - 1

It is good to question.

I have many questions about trust.

~ Do I want to trust anyone?

~ Why would I trust anyone?

~ Will it help me heal if I trust another?

~ Whom can I trust?

~ What is trustworthy about me?

~ Does anyone trust me?   Why?

Today I will choose two of these questions and answer them in writing or by creating an image.

expression

3 Trust

Rebuilding Trust - 2

Today I will sit silently for 5 minutes and think of someone I trust.

When I am ready I write about why I trust this person or I create an image of how I feel trusting this person.

or -

If no one comes to mind whom I feel I can trust, I write or create an image about how I might feel if I trusted someone.

expression

32

Rebuilding Trust - 3

*T*oday I want to identify a safe place.

I sit quietly, close my eyes and imagine myself in a safe place.

This may be where I am sitting right now or a place in my mind.

As I sit, I notice the sights, sounds, smells and feel of this place of safety. I think about the colors and notice if anyone else is there as I visualize, feel, know or sense this safe place.

Remaining quiet with my eyes closed, I pay attention to how my body feels in this safe place.

When I am ready I open my eyes and write about or create an image of this experience.

or -

If I am uncomfortable closing my eyes and imagining a safe place, I can simply sit in silence for 5 minutes.

When I am ready I write about or create an image of my safe place.

expression

3 Trust

Rebuilding Trust - Spiritual Expression

Sometimes

~ it is hard to believe I can trust something greater than myself.

~ it is difficult for me to believe in goodness.

~ I wonder why and how the abuse happened.

~ I want to believe in something beyond myself.

~ I want to believe in a Supreme Being.

Today I write or create an image about how my ability or desire to trust in something greater than myself was affected by the abuse.

or-

I write two or more affirmations about learning to trust in something greater than myself.

spiritual
expression

Trust and Feelings

I am not always aware of what I feel.

I don't always know what my emotions are.

Sometimes, while the abuse occurred
~ I numbed out.
~ I disconnected from my feelings.
~ I left my body.
~ I stayed in a small spot on the ceiling.

As I begin to heal,
~ I do not always know my feelings.
~ I do not always want to speak my feelings.
~ I still feel numb and cut off from myself.

Healing, I am learning,
~ to stay with the feelings in my body.
~ to trust my body and myself.
~ to slowly let go of the numbing process.
~ to say what I feel.
~ to trust others with my feelings.

As I leave the systems of exploitation and abuse behind me,
~ I learn how I feel,
~ I speak how I feel,
~ I enjoy how I feel.

r e a d i n g

3 Trust

Trust And Feelings - 1

Today I will be aware of how I feel while events are occurring. In addition to times of quiet or calm I note if and when I numb out. (Numb out is to ignore or stop feeling).

At the end of the day I pick two or more situations and note how I felt.

For example:

Disagreement with co-worker; angry then numbed out.

Reading after dinner; peaceful, content.

expression

36

Trust And Feelings - 2

Numbing out was once a way I stayed safe. I did not want to feel while the abuse happened. To feel and to talk about how I felt was dangerous. There are times, even as I recover, that it still seems dangerous for me to feel and to talk about how I feel.

As I recover I ask myself

~ What is it like to want to feel?

~ What is it like for me to feel again?

~ Can I stop numbing out?

~ What is it like for me to remember how I felt?

~ What is it like to share how I feel now?

~ What is it like to share how I felt during the abuse?

I give myself permission to explore trusting my feelings.

I choose two or more of the questions above and write in response to them.

or -

I create an image as I read through the questions.

expression

3 *Trust*

Trust And Feelings - 3

I trust myself more if I have a sense of affection for myself.

Sitting silently, I bring to mind a time when I felt warm, cared for or comforted. This may have been a time I was outside, alone in my room or with a friend. I allow myself to feel the warmth and affection.

~ What images pass through my mind?

~ What feelings arise?

I create an image or write about these feelings of affection.

expression

38

Trust And Feelings - Spiritual Expression

To learn to feel, I need to feel safe. I need to learn that I can be comforted, even while experiencing difficult and frightening feelings.

I create an image of safety. I want my image to convey a sense of comfort and well being. When I feel sad, scared, anxious, frightened, when I want to numb out, I can bring to mind my image of comfort.

or -

I can call and get some ideas about what images my support people use when frightened, sad or anxious. I write down the ideas from my support person.

spiritual expression

3 Trust

Discovering And Setting Boundaries

When I was abused; my trust was destroyed as my physical, mental, emotional and spiritual boundaries were invaded. Learning to trust myself I establish boundaries and private space in my life.

I am learning that I can set limits and
    boundaries
        ~on how I am touched,
        ~ on my thoughts,
        ~ on my feelings.

I can choose
        ~ what spiritual tradition I want to
        create in my life.

I can say
        ~ No, that doesn't work for me.
        ~ Do not touch me.
        ~ I do not want to talk about that right
        now.

Discovering and creating boundaries
    empowers me.
        ~ I am empowered as I start to trust
        myself.
        ~ I am empowered when I recognize my
        limits.
        ~ I am empowered when I establish
        boundaries.
        ~ I am empowered when I tell others
        what my boundaries are.
        ~ I am empowered as I establish private
        space for myself.

reading

Discovering And Setting Boundaries - 1

Part of trusting myself is setting limits. Part of setting limits is learning to say NO. Saying NO when it is in my best interest to say NO facilitates learning to trust myself. Learning to say NO in difficult times and places is part of my recovery.

As I grow I can practice saying NO.

To learn how to say NO I can watch a two year old say no.

I can learn to say NO without apology.

I can learn to say NO without guilt.

Today I set some limits. I practice saying NO one to three times today.

I pay attention to how I feel as I say NO.

I write or create an image of myself as I learn to say NO.

expression

Discovering And Setting Boundaries - 2

*I*ncest and sexual exploitation are usually secrets. I was told (directly or indirectly) not to speak of what happened. This meant keeping a secret that was dangerous to me. This confused me. Sometimes I wanted to talk about what was happening but I trusted the perpetrator and did not speak.

As I heal I learn to trust myself. I learn to trust my inner knowledge. I learn to trust my own inner voices.

I am learning

~ I can choose to talk about the abuse.

~ I can choose to talk with whom I wish about the abuse.

~ I can choose when, where and how I will talk.

~ I can choose to be silent.

I feel empowered

~ when I decide what I am going to say,

~ when I discover and set boundaries.

I make three lists:

1. A list of one or more secrets about the abuse.

2. A list naming secrets I HAVE talked about as I heal.

3. A list naming the secrets I HAVE NOT yet talked about but wish to.

Completing my lists I can decide if, when, where and with whom I wish to talk about these secrets.

expression

Discovering And Setting Boundaries - 3

*B*lurts Disease...that awful time when I have said more than I wanted, or said something and later wished I had not said anything.

I find myself blurting things out

~ to strangers.

~ to people I do not trust.

~ to people who are unsafe for me.

~ at inappropriate times.

As I heal I find that blurting things out

~ is often a part of healing.

~ may mean I need to find someone safe to talk with.

~ may mean I need to go to a support meeting.

~ may mean I have things I need to say.

~ may mean there are things I want to say.

Today I write down the names and phone numbers of a person or people with whom I feel safe, people I trust. I list phone numbers of helplines. I flag this page of my workbook. When I want a phone number I can find this page with ease.

expression

3 Trust

Discovering And Setting Boundaries - Spiritual Expression

Supreme Being, God or something greater than myself is often portrayed as all-knowing and all seeing. Sometimes this is frightening because it seems I have no privacy and no control about my relationship with God. Abuse by someone with a religious affiliation such as a priest, nun or minister, may increase my sense of oppression and fear about something greater than myself.

Though it is contrary to some religious traditions, as a survivor, *I get* to be in charge of how, if and when I engage in a relationship with something greater than myself. Learning to trust my own spiritual tradition I get to set boundaries and limits. In this way I begin to reclaim my private space and the boundaries of my spiritual tradition.

Today I write a letter. In my letter I state what kind of relationship I want to have with a Supreme Being. (Keep in mind this may mean no relationship at this time).

*spiritual
expression*

44

Grief and Loss

"I have had to give up everything I have ever known in order to recover. I lost over thirty years of a life I now know I never had. How can I ever be consoled?"

Survivor

4

4 Grief and Loss

Naming My Losses

Facing losses every day

I struggle,
I feel overwhelmed.

I name my losses.
I have lost
~ confidence,
~ hope,
~ creativity,
~ curiosity.
I have lost
~ self-esteem,
~ self-acceptance,
~ creativity.
I have lost
~ family,
~ friends,
~ time,
~ money,
~ energy.
I have lost faith in my God.

As I name my losses, talk with others, cry
with others I learn that

~ there is more than just loss.
~ I can grow beyond my losses.

reading

Naming My Losses - 1

As I heal I name my losses.

I have losses -

~ I felt as a child.

~ I felt during the abuse.

~ I felt as I better understood the abuse.

~ I feel now.

Today I name my losses and the feelings with the losses.

For example:

Losses include my time and energy for hobbies and projects.

My feelings about this are anger, sadness, betrayal and hurt.

expression

Naming My Losses - 2

When I am aware of my losses I need comfort.

How can I comfort myself when I grieve?

~ Call on another?

~ Sit wrapped in a blanket?

~ Go to a movie?

~ Take a hot bath?

~ Go to a support group meeting?

~ Talk to my pet?

How can others comfort me when I grieve?

~ Remain silent and listen?

~ Talk with me?

~ Hold me?

I do deserve comfort as I grieve. I will create an image or write answers to one or two of these questions.

or -

I write my thoughts about comfort and grief in my life.

expression

Naming My Losses - 3

Talking with others about the losses from the sexual abuse,

> I affirm that there is more than loss in my life.
> I affirm a connection with others,
> I affirm that my life grows beyond abuse.

As I heal I find other survivors and
~I talk about losses.
~I share my feelings about my losses.
~I ask about coping skills.
~I talk about my needs as I grieve.

I talk with one other person about my losses, my griefs.

I write about this experience on this page.

or -

If I am not ready to talk with another, I write about or create an image of how I might feel sharing my grief.

expression

Naming My Losses - Spiritual Expression

I want to believe that there is something greater than myself in the universe. I feel abandoned and betrayed by God. How could the abuse have happened to me?

Today I write a letter to something/someone greater than myself.

In my letter, I describe my grief, loss, sense of abandonment.

I speak about what I need and want in a relationship with my God.

spiritual
expression

My Tears Are Healing

Tears are part of healing from sexual abuse.
My heart opens as I allow myself to weep.

Sometimes
- ~ I weep inside.
- ~ I can not weep.
- ~ I am lonely when I cry.

I am learning
- ~ to allow myself the release of tears.
- ~ to be gentle with myself when I cry.
- ~ that healing is sharing my tears.
- ~ that a witness to my tears lets me
  share my pain.

reading

My Tears Are Healing - 1

What can I tell myself about my tears? Can I learn about tears from my support group? Are there times when my tears flow more readily? Are there times when my tears do not come at all?

On this page I can safely write about or create an image of my feelings about tears.

expression

My Tears Are Healing - 2

I know that not all my tears show on the
outside.

Sometimes

~ I have inner tears.

~ my tears are inside.

I create an image of my inner tears.

If I choose, I may share this image with a
support person.

Reaching out, I remind myself that tears are a
part of healing and that I am not alone.

expression

My Tears Are Healing - 3

When am I comfortable with my tears?
When am I not?

How can I be comforted while I weep?

What is this image for me?

Might I ask another to comfort me?

In my quiet time today I reflect on these questions. I create an image or write in response to these questions.

expression

54

My Tears Are Healing -
Spiritual Expression

As I sit and listen to soft music, I allow
images of my tears healing me to form.

I create an image of these tears.

*spiritual
expression*

4 Grief and Loss

Discoveries About Grief

Because I am a survivor of sexual abuse I grieve.

I have sustained many losses.

~ My tears do not measure my deep, deep grief.
~ I have not words for my grief.
~ I keen, moan and weep.
~ I rock, and rock and weep.
~ I hold myself and weep.

Each day, I am aware of another loss.

Giving myself permission to grieve, I experience at full range feelings of sorrow, hurt, pain, loss, despair and sadness.
~ I do not have to stop my feelings any longer.
~ I am free to grieve.
~ I am free to move beyond the grief of being sexually abused.

reading

Discoveries About Grief - 1

How do I grieve? Do I cry? Wail? Soundlessly weep?

~ Cry at movies?

~ Laugh when I want to cry?

~ Clench my teeth so I don't cry?

~ Feel angry but not sad?

~ Keep too busy?

~ Push friends away?

How do I grieve? Do I pretend I don't have grief?

~ Do I cry and wonder if I will ever stop?

~ Do I write letters?

~ Do I try to talk to others?

~ How do others grieve?

Taking some time to reflect on how I grieve, I write about or create an image in response to two or more of these questions.

expression

Discoveries About Grief - 2

Loss
~ a legacy of the abuse.
My life
~ irrevocably altered.

Sitting in silence I list the ways my life has been changed.

For example:

~ I have lost -
~ I feel empty of -

When I am finished, I take time to get connected with the present.

I look about the room and remember I am moving beyond the abuse.

expression

Discoveries About Grief - 3

What stops me from grieving?

What messages do I have that prevent me from grieving?

What do I say to myself when I experience sorrow, sadness, loss and despair?

What could I say to myself?

What would encourage my grief? My grieving?

Taking some quiet time for myself, I respond by creating an image or writing about two of these questions.

or -

In my quiet time I write about how grieving can help my recovery process.

expression

Discoveries About Grief - Spiritual Expression

Death is acknowledged with memorial services and funerals.

Comfort and support are given to the bereaved. The grief of sexual abuse and exploitation is not often acknowledged.

Today I acknowledge my losses. How can I do this?

~ Can I play some music and light a candle?

~ Can I make a list of my losses and destroy the list?

~ Can I write down my losses and share my list with my support people?

During my time for myself I can decide and write down how I will acknowledge my losses. Setting aside the time I need, I follow through on my ideas. I note how I felt.

or -

If I am not ready to actually take some time for myself, I can write about or create an image of how I would like to acknowledge my losses.

spiritual
expression

As I Grieve, Life Returns

I am a survivor.

I thought the pain would be over if I lived
    through the abuse.

I thought I would be finished saying
    good-bye to my nightmares
        ~ when the abuse ended.

Now I find this isn't true.
    ~ I have this enormous feeling of
      emptiness inside me.
    ~ I feel blank and alone.

I have lost so much.
    ~ I have lost the ability to trust.
    ~ I was raped of my childhood,
  ~my innocence was destroyed.
    ~ I feel like I will be alone forever.
    ~ I am afraid of the dark.
    ~ I don't sleep through the night.
    ~ I wake up weeping.

I want to stop the grief.
I want to feel full inside.
I want to feel connected to others.
I want my grief to stop.
I have survived.
Now I grieve.
As I grieve
    ~ Life returns.

reading

4 Grief and Loss

As I Grieve, Life Returns - 1

The losses I experience from sexual abuse are numerous. Giving myself permission to grieve, I acknowledge the process of healing.

Closing my eyes, sitting in silence and becoming still, I allow an image of my grief to form in my mind.

I create this image of my grief and note how I felt about this exercise.

expression

As I Grieve, Life Returns - 2

What is it like for me to lose my ability to trust others?

How do I grieve the lack of trust?

Who can I trust today with my losses?

I find some colored pencils and create an image or write about one or more of these questions. I let the colors and the words or images express my feelings.

expression

4 Grief and Loss

As I Grieve, Life Returns - 3

Dreaming and creating new ideas, thoughts and activities are part of life. Sexual abuse and exploitation have a crippling effect on dreams and ideas.

I ask myself

~ What dreams did I give up as a result of the abuse?

~ How do I feel about this loss of dreams?

~ How have my dreams changed?

~ What do I dream now?

Today I respond to two or more of these questions.

or -

I create an image or write about my dreams.

As I heal my dreams can become realities.

expression

As I Grieve, Life Returns -
Spiritual Expression

How does sharing my grief connect me to others?

How does joy come into my life as I grieve?

What do I gain from sharing and expressing my grief?

How does expressing my grief connect me to my own experiences of healing and coming back to myself?

Today I create images or write about one or two of these questions.

spiritual expression

Anger

"I want to get
angry
I want to get mad
I want to get angry
And not feel so
sad...

Your sorrows were
yours
You made them
mine
I want to get angry
Just for one
time..."

From *The Angry
Song*

5 Anger

Learning to Express My Anger

I feel angry that I was sexually abused and I
am learning to express that rage.

I am aware that sometimes
- I feel a surge of angry or rageful
  feelings.
- some of my angry feelings are so
  intense that I feel frightened.
- I have fantasies and thoughts that are
  destructive or hurtful toward others
  or myself.
- I feel like I'm being consumed.
- I do not always know what to do.

I am learning
- that I do not need to destroy myself
  or others when I am angry.
- I can express my feelings of rage and
  anger in ways that are respectful to
  myself and others.
- that my anger does not consume me.
- I do not need to act on those
  negative thoughts and fantasies.
- I am in CHARGE of my anger!

reading

68

5 | Anger

Learning To Express My Anger - 1

I am learning to name, feel and express my anger and rage.

I find that sometimes I have fearful feelings about my anger.

When I acknowledge that I am afraid I may get out of control with my angry feelings, or that I may want to hurt someone else or myself, I can start to free myself from my fear about anger.

Today I choose one of the following:

I write down my fears about my angry, rageful feelings.

or -

I create an image of my fear about my anger and rage.

or -

I jot down a few of the reasons I do not like to get angry.

expression

5 Anger

Learning To Express My Anger - 2

I am learning to express my anger and rage.

Today

~ I talk with another person about anger.

~ I may choose to talk with a support person, a group member, another survivor, a helping professional or a friend.

~ I ask one of these people about coping with angry feelings.

~ I may talk about my own angry feelings.

I write down how I felt talking about anger and rage.

expression

Learning To Express My Anger - 3

Closing my eyes and becoming still I bring to mind a SMALL memory or situation about which I feel angry. I pay attention to my body.

~ Where, in my body, do I feel my anger?

~ How does my body feel when I am angry?

~ Do my angry feelings travel throughout my body or do they remain in one area?

Opening my eyes I draw an outline of my body.

Within the outline I note the places in my body I hold my anger.

Once my drawing is complete I find a safe way to release the anger.

~ I may choose to walk, run, paint, talk out loud to myself,

~ scream silently, break sticks or tear paper. (preferably not this workbook!)

I WILL NOT HARM MYSELF OR ANOTHER.

After I have drawn the picture, and worked with my anger, I write down how I felt doing this exercise.

expression

5 Anger

Learning To Express My Anger - Spiritual Expression

Anger can be turned into a productive tool. Today I list ways that my anger can be transformed.

I may work in the garden, take a brisk walk, attend to my health.

I may take a warm bath, listen to music or talk with another survivor and tell my story.

How can I transform some of my anger into something productive in my life?

In my workbook I write about or create an image of transforming my anger into something productive and life giving.

spiritual
expression

72

Changing My Views About Anger

My family had rules about anger.
   Lots of rules.
      ~ Some of the rules were spoken.
      ~ Some of the rules were not spoken.

Some of those rules were:
      ~ Do not get angry, get even.
      ~ Children do not get angry.
      ~ Anger is a bad thing, do not be
         angry.
      ~ Do not get angry with family
         members.
      ~ Getting mad means getting punished.
      ~ When someone gets mad, someone
         gets hurt.

Sometimes, in the past, anger and rage were
   violently expressed.
Sometimes, in the past, anger and rage were
   sexually expressed.

I have a deep rage about being abused.
Sometimes it feels very powerful. Too
   powerful to give voice to.
I am frightened, sometimes, by my rage.
      ~ I hold my rage in my body.
      ~ I hold my rage in my mind.
      ~ I hold my rage in my heart.
      ~ I do not speak or express my rage.

I want to move that anger to constructive
   channels.
I do not want to be a container of anger any
   longer.
I want to be free of the oppressive weight of
   my rage.
I want my anger to free me.
I want the productive energy of my anger to
   heal me.

reading

5 Anger

Changing My Views About Anger - 1

My family had rules about anger, about rage.

~ What were the rules in my family?

~ What were the verbal rules? the non-verbal rules?

~ What did I learn about anger in my family?

As I reflect on one or more of these questions I write about or create an image.

expression

Changing My Views About Anger - 2

Sometimes
My anger feels HUGE.

The power of my anger frightens me.

I feel so angry, I feel destructive.

I don't want to hurt myself or someone else.

I need someone I can talk to when I am
angry.

With whom can I talk?

Today I list the names and phone numbers of
one or more support people, or potential
support people, who could help me when I
feel angry or destructive. I might include
helpline phone numbers, support people,
friends and helping professionals. As I am
ready, I can call the persons on this list
when I need support.

expression

5 Anger

Changing My Views About Anger - 3

My goal is to live through my anger, to express my anger beneficially for me and not to hurt myself or another.

Clay, paint, crayons, large pieces of newsprint, construction paper can all be used when I feel angry.

I can channel my anger by:

~ Molding the clay and throwing it at newsprint covered walls;

~ Painting with large strokes;

~ Coloring, with force, on large pieces of paper;

~ Painting images of my anger;

~ Sculpting images from clay and then punching them back to whatever shape I wish;

~ Drawing on newsprint and then tearing up the newsprint;

~ Ripping and pasting construction paper into images of anger;

I create an image of my anger using materials available to me.

I call a person from my support list when I have completed this activity. In this manner I stay connected to my support community when I have angry feelings.

expression

76

Changing My Views About Anger - Spiritual Expression

There are myriad ways to view something greater than myself.

Some belief systems allow for an angry God, but not angry believers.

Sometimes those who have been sexually abused by people with religious affiliation have many feelings of betrayal and anger toward a Supreme Being.

What are my beliefs about being angry with something greater than myself?

~ Am I angry with my Higher Power?

~ Is a Supreme Being angry with me?

~ Am I being punished?

~ If God is not angry, why did this happen?

~ How do I reconcile my feelings of anger and betrayal with God?

Giving myself permission to explore this topic, I create an image of whatever develops from these questions and images.

spiritual expression

5 Anger

My Anger Empowers Me

Sometimes
~ I feel full of rage.
~ I do not always know how to cope
with my anger and rage.
~ I turn my anger inward, harming
myself.
~ I do not eat right, I drink to excess, I
isolate.

~ I do not know how to be angry and
not hurt myself.
~ I want to harm others or go after the
perpetrator.

I have seen men lash out at women.
I have seen enraged women hit children.
I wonder how I can express my rage.

Today I am learning
~ that I can live through my anger.
~ to deal with my anger in healthy
ways.
~ I have choices about acting out my
anger.
~ I can turn my anger into
empowerment.

reading

78

My Anger Empowers Me - 1

I have choices about how to use my anger to empower me.

I can use suggestions from the reading.

I can talk with someone.

I can learn about my choices by

~ talking with my support people,

~ talking with helping professionals,

~ reading about anger,

~ calling a helpline.

I list some choices I have about how I use anger to empower me. I may also list some people who can help me with my angry feelings.

expression

79

5 Anger

My Anger Empowers Me - 2

I am angry about being sexually abused. Listing the abusive acts that enrage me helps me feel some of my anger.

Today I list one or more of the abusive acts about which I am angry. This is an act of empowerment.

I can read my list to

~ my professional helpers,

~ a support group,

~ a supportive friend.

or -

If I am not ready to speak to others I will read the list to myself as an affirmation that my anger is empowering to me.

expression

My Anger Empowers Me - 3

Anger is a physical as well as emotional response. I feel it in my body as well as my heart. During the abuse I did not know what to do with the anger I was feeling in my body.

Sometimes when I am angry I have physical responses.
  My heart pounds.
  I start to sweat.
  My stomach knots up.

Sometimes when memories return I have physical responses.
  I feel sick to my stomach.
  I have headaches.
  I want to sleep.

As I heal I
~ feel my anger in my body,
~ let my anger bubble out of my body,
~ allow myself to express the anger I feel.
~ learn to be angry with others, but not harm them or myself.

Today, expressing my anger I can:
~ walk fast while speaking aloud my angry feelings,
~ run, play racquetball, swim,
~ mow my lawn, dig out weeds, prune a hedge,
~ draw or write in my journal,
~ tear newspapers or phone books.

If I am ready and have my list of support people at hand, I choose one way to physically express my anger. For 10 minutes I express myself physically. After 10 minutes I write in my workbook how I felt and I call a support person.

expression

5 Anger

My Anger Empowers Me -
Spiritual Expression

Standing on solid ground I feel the earth
support me.

Standing solid on the earth my anger reminds
me of a storm; it surges through me and I
feel cleansed by the rains.

The flashes of lightning remind me of my
powerful anger.

Sitting quietly I allow images of anger to form
in my mind. I create one or more of these
images.

or -

If no image comes to mind I write about what
in nature reminds me of my anger.

*spiritual
expression*

Self Esteem

> "I used to think I was nothing. As I've healed, I've begun to feel more powerful, but it's slow going. I am terrified and angry that I had to wait until my mid-thirties to even begin to know that I was someone."

Survivor

6

Taking Care Of My Needs

In a sexually abusive relationship

I learned that
- ~ what I wanted, the abuse to stop, did not matter.
- ~ what I cared about, feeling safe and protected, did not matter.
- ~ who I was, someone vulnerable, did not matter.

I want to learn
- ~ to know what I want.
- ~ to ask for what I want.
- ~ to joyfully accept.
- ~ to give when I want to give.

Ways I might take care of my needs:
- ~ educate myself about sexual abuse and exploitation,
- ~ ask questions,
- ~ talk with others,
- ~ talk with other survivors,
- ~ speak my truth.

I might take care of myself by
- ~ finding out if there are professionals, in my location, who are trained to work with survivors of sexual exploitation and abuse.

Other ways I can take care of my needs are to eat well, exercise, rest and play.

As I learn to find my inner harmony, a natural balance evolves in my life.

reading

Taking Care Of My Needs - 1

Healing, I discover lots of needs and wants for my life.

I list my needs and wants and note how to get them met.

Do I need the support of a group?
I can visit support groups to find ones I like.

Do I need more time to myself?
I can find 15 minutes a day for me.

Do I need more play or music in my life?
I can get a new tape that makes me feel good.

Do I need to get connected to other survivors?
I can call a helpline and check out resources.

Do I need to have more fun?
I can call a friend and make plans to get together.

In the space below I name my needs and write how I can get these needs met.

expression

Taking Care Of My Needs - 2

When I began my recovery I was surprised and dismayed to discover that the memories and feelings I experienced left me feeling small, weak and vulnerable.

As I heal

~ I learn how to take care of myself when I am vulnerable.

~ I begin to understand how destructive the abuse was.

~ I learn to be gentle with myself when memories return.

~ I learn to stay connected to my support groups.

In the space below I write down what I need when I am feeling small and vulnerable.

For example:
    Call a support person,
    Write gentle words,
    Envision my support group aiding me.

expression

Taking Care Of My Needs - 3

Balance is important in my life. My needs were ignored when I was sexually abused. Learning to balance my needs and wants with those of another is an important step in recovery. I start to look at balancing my needs and the needs of others in my life by focusing on one or two of my closest relationships.

In the space below I write about one or more of the following questions.

~ Do both of us give something?

~ Am I afraid to state my needs?

~ Are my wishes sometimes fulfilled?

~ How do I take care of myself in this relationship?

~ Does the relationship encourage self care for both people?

~ Are any of my relationships exploitative?

~ Are any of my relationships sexually abusive?

~ Am I aware of any patterns that concern me?

~ What does a balanced relationship mean to me?

expression

Taking Care Of My Needs - Spiritual Expression

*D*reaming about how I want my life to be is part of self-care.

Today I will dream about

~ a vacation - a trip to Hawaii,

~ a time in the woods,

~ being in a healthy relationship,

~ going to school,

~ a new job that is exciting,

~ a colorful wardrobe,

~ planting a wild flower garden.

Today is DREAM DAY.

As part of DREAM DAY I write about or create images of my dreams in the space below. When I have finished I close my eyes and imagine my dreams happening.

spiritual expression

Ways to Nurture Myself

Do I nurture myself?

Do I allow others to nurture me?
Sometimes
~ I resist the idea of nurturing.
~ it is difficult for me to receive
warmth or kindness.
~ I believe I do not deserve to care for
myself.
~ I do not believe that I deserve the
care of others.

Can I
~ talk about my fear of receiving
warmth and kindness?
~ learn to accept a friend's offer of
empathy and support?
~ read or talk about how sexual abuse
effects my ability to receive?

As I talk with others my fears begin to
dissipate and I discover that
~ nurturing is an acceptable and
necessary part of life.
~ I feel lighter in spirit as I open up to
others.

I embrace the idea that there are many ways
to nurture myself.
I learn that there are many ways to be
nurtured.
I embrace that idea that I can nurture others.

r e a d i n g

6 *Self Esteem*

Ways to Nurture Myself - 1

I talk to some support people and find out
ways they nurture themselves. I jot down
what I learned about how others nurture
themselves. I put a star (*) by any ideas I
like.

expression

Ways To Nurture Myself - 2

Today I find a comfortable place to sit and relax. I turn on soothing and relaxing music and imagine ways to further nurture myself.

Today I might imagine

~ getting flowers from a friend or family member.

~ healing from the abuse.

~ playing basketball with friends.

~ talking to others.

I write about or create an image of one or more ways I imagined being nurtured.

expression

Ways To Nurture Myself - 3

Fearful thoughts and feelings get in the way of nurturing myself.

Naming my fears loosens the hold my fears have on me.

I am learning that even if I am frightened it is okay for me to

~ receive care from others.

~ find ways to nurture myself.

~ ask for comfort and reassurance.

~ make a firm step in my recovery.

What is it about nurturing that frightens me?

Today I start to identify those things which frighten me.

I write down the fears I identify.

A couple of examples are:

I feel fearful when others nurture me because I am afraid I will be tricked.

I keep too busy to slow down and nurture myself because I am afraid that if I take time for myself, painful feelings will surface.

expression

Ways To Nurture Myself -
Spiritual Expression

Planting trees.

Working in the garden.

Walking barefoot in the sand.

Walking in the grass.

Touching the drops of a gentle rain.

Watching the sunset or sunrise.

Feeling the warmth of the sun.

Playing in the snow.

All can be nourishing and nurturing.

Today I either sit outside or just imagine
myself outside.

In my workbook I note what feels nurturing
to me.

I create an image of what nurtures me.

*spiritual
expression*

6 Self Esteem

My Needs Are Important

I was sexually abused. While this happened
I was learning
> ~ that my needs were not important.
> ~ that the needs of the perpetrator
> came first.

My needs
> ~ were not met,
> ~ were not considered,
> ~ were cast aside,
> ~ were invisible.

In my childhood I learned
> ~ not to speak my needs.
> ~ not to acknowledge my needs.
> ~ not to ask for my needs to be met.
> ~ not to expect my needs to be
> addressed.

Even as I heal I hear the messages
> ~ I better not expect much.
> ~ I should not ask for much.
> ~ my needs are not important.
> ~ I am afraid that no one really cares
> anyway.
> ~ I will not ask for too much.

As I grow beyond the abuse I realize that
> ~ My needs are important to me.
> ~ I can say what I need.
> ~ I can be realistic about my needs.
> ~ Others may want to meet my needs.

r e a d i n g

My Needs Are Important - 1

I learned, from the abuse, that my needs were not important. My needs were not considered.

~ What needs were these?

~ My need for privacy?

~ My need to control what happened to my body?

~ My need to be respected?

I write about which needs of mine were not met and how this affects me today.

or -

I create a list of my needs. I write some ideas about how to get one or more of these needs met.

expression

My Needs Are Important - 2

As a child my needs were not met. When I was sexually exploited my needs were not met.

I was not considered.

I was not protected.

I was not safe.

I was not heard.

As I recover I begin to meet these needs.

Today I write about or create an image of how I take care of my inner child or the exploited parts of myself.

For example:

I protect my child by talking with safe people.

If I wish, I ask a support person to listen to what I have written or show them my created image.

expression

My Needs Are Important - 3

As I heal I learn to ask others to meet some of my needs.

~ I need to know that others are also healing.

~ I need to be heard as I tell my story.

~ I need support when I am fearful or angry.

~ I need to share laughter and tears with others.

I can, and will, learn to ask to get my needs met. When it is helpful for me I ask other survivors, friends, helping professional and/or my partner to meet my needs.

My needs will not always be met. Communication skills aid me as I learn to ask for my needs. I can negotiate, listen to the other person, change the way I ask for the need to be met or ask another to meet the need.

Today I write down communication skills I have that assist me as I learn to ask others to meet my needs.

For example:

Writing out what I want, then asking for it.

I am a good listener.

expression

6 *Self Esteem*

My Needs Are Important - Spiritual Expression

During the time I was abused my needs were secondary to the perpetrator's needs. Learning to balance getting my needs met and meeting the needs of another, in a healthy way, is important.

As I heal I am learning that when I give to another, some of my needs are met. These might be needs for self esteem, confidence, inclusiveness, enjoyment and self expression. I am also learning that I cannot give to someone else and ignore my own needs.

I can ask others which needs of theirs are met when they give to another and how they take care of themselves.

Today I write any thoughts I have about how I take care of myself and give to another.

or -

I create an image of myself giving to another.

*spiritual
expression*

Accountability

"Any therapist who establishes sexual contact with a patient should be sued for malpractice and prosecuted for statutory rape."

Dr. William Masters, M.D.
(Masters and Johnson)
December 21, 1990

"If I had not learned that the perpetrator was, and could be made, accountable for destroying my ability to trust God, myself, and others, I would not be here today!"

Survivor

7

7 Accountability

Through the Silence I Speak

Often as I heal from the sexual abuse I find
myself silent.

Sometimes
~ I retreat to a shell of silent darkness.
~ I do not want to speak with anyone.

The darkness is familiar, and sometimes,
comforting to me.

I am learning
~ that the dark silence is not always so
welcoming.
~ that speaking does not have to mean
betrayal or further abuse.
~ that speaking to others is helpful.
~ that telling my story is one way to
promote healing.

At times I still retreat to silence and wrap
the darkness around me.
Moving through the silences, starting to tell
my story, I continue to heal.

reading

Through the Silence I Speak - 1

*T*oday I become aware of times I am silent.

I reflect on these questions:

~ Why do I choose to be silent? When am I silent?

~ What do I receive from the silence?

~ Is my silence healing? Why or Why not? When is it healing?

Today I create an image or write about my silence.

expression

7 Accountability

Through The Silence
I Speak - 2

There were layers of secrecy with the abuse. I had to keep secrets, other people's secrets. I kept secrets, sometimes for years. The secrets were harmful, binding, destructive and crippling to me.

As I heal I learn that I want *privacy* in my life, not secrets. I want to have choice and freedom about what I say and to whom. I want to be silent when I choose. I want to speak when it is helpful and respectful to myself.

Today I create two images.

On a separate piece of paper I create an image of myself with the secrets of the abuse. Next to this image I write words that remind me of those secrets.

I create a second image of myself on this page. This is an image of myself with privacy. Next to this image I write words that mean private, free, choice, whole.

or~

I may write about one of more of these questions.

~ How do I feel about privacy instead of secrecy in my life?
~ When do I have secrets?
~ When am I private?

expression

Through The Silence
I Speak - 3

Today I list the names of people or a person to whom I can tell my story. These are people who have not betrayed my trust.

I look at the person(s) named and I answer one or more of the following questions:

~ Why is this person safe?

~ Will I tell my whole story?

~ Can I tell a part of my story?

~ How do I feel as I start to tell my story?

If there is no one in my life that I want to trust right now I write about how telling my story could enhance my recovery.

expression

7 Accountability

Through The Silence
I Speak- Spiritual Expression

*T*oday I tell my story to a Supreme Being.

I write what I would tell the Supreme Being
  if we were face to face.

What happens inside of me as I tell my story?

spiritual
expression

I Did Not Cause The Abuse

Sometimes
~ I think I am made of inferior parts.
~ I tell myself I should have known
better.
~ I tell myself I should have been able
to stop the abuse.
~ I believe I caused the abuse, that I am
no good.

I am changing
~ my negative thinking a little each
day,
~ and letting go of crippling beliefs that
I caused the abuse.

I am learning
~ to see myself as worthwhile.
~ to treat myself with kindness.
~ that I am whole and full of goodness.

r e a d i n g

7 Accountability

I Did Not Cause The Abuse - 1

I am changing some of the negative beliefs I learned about myself.

Reaching out to others, doing some research, I find that other survivors may have felt as I do.

To find if others have felt like I do I could

~ Call a local or national helpline.

~ Call a member of my support or friendship group.

~ Check out a self help book on abuse.

Some questions I might want to ask are:

~ Did other survivors ever think they caused the abuse?

~ Are other survivors afraid to talk about the abuse?

I note in my workbook how I felt asking other survivors if they had negative beliefs similar to mine.

expression

I Did Not Cause The Abuse - 2

In my past
~ I learned to believe that I caused the horrible things that happened to me.

~ I thought I was responsible for the happiness of the adults around me.

~ I believed that I caused the abuse.

Today I look in a mirror, and say aloud three times
I DID NOT CAUSE THE SEXUAL ABUSE.

I write
I DID NOT CAUSE THE SEXUAL ABUSE.

I note how I feel about saying and writing this sentence.

expression

107

I Did Not Cause The Abuse - 3

Shame - that big, dark, oily, awful feeling I get. It's so easy to feel and so hard to get rid of.

I had hoped that

~ my feelings of shame would go away as soon as I started recovery.

~ my negative thoughts about myself would immediately cease.

~ I wouldn't feel shameful anymore.

Instead I find myself feeling shameful when I

~ make a mistake.

~ talk about the abuse.

~ talk about my sexuality.

~ feel certain feelings (anger, grief, rage).

Today I create two images, one of myself feeling shame and another image of myself free from the shame. As I compare the images I note what I learn about myself from these two images.

expression

I Did Not Cause The
Abuse - Spiritual Expression

Slowing down and getting centered helps me remember I did not cause the abuse. As I heal I learn to slow down, to calm myself.

Today
I close my eyes and become still. I breathe deeply, all the way to my feet. I imagine I am sitting beside a deep, clear, still lake. I hold the image of the calm lake in my mind. I relax into the calm, stillness the lake provides.

While feeling calm, centered, grounded, I remind myself
    ~ I am valuable,
    ~I am joyful,
    ~ I am creative.
I note in my workbook how I felt with this exercise and ways I can calm myself during each day.

spiritual
expression

7 *Accountability*

Standing My Ground

Sometimes I find myself thinking:

> ~ I am responsible.
> ~ I could have stopped the abuse.
> ~ I made the perpetrator hurt me
>   because
> > I was too noticeable,
> > I was there.

Sometimes messages from the abuser run
through my head:
> ~ "You will like this." "You will feel
>   better."
> ~ "I will not hurt you."
> ~ "I'm only teaching you what you will
>   need to know."
> ~ "You asked for this."
> ~ "I am attracted to you."
> ~ "You are special."
> ~ "I've never felt this way about
>   anyone else."

Sometimes
> ~ I feel frightened, stuck and isolated.
> ~ I remember how I felt
>   late at night in my bedroom,
>   alone in the office, no one there.
> ~ I wonder can I just let this go?

As I talk with other survivors and
professionals
> ~ I hear them say that:
> > I am not responsible for the
> > abuse.
> > I did not cause the abuse.
> > I could not stop the abuse.

I want to believe they are right.
I hope they are correct.

Gradually, like dawn breaking, I start to
believe what I hear.

I start to believe my innocence.

r e a d i n g

110

Standing My Ground - 1

Some days messages from the person who abused me stay in my mind.

The messages are deadly

~ I wanted to be abused.

~ I am responsible for the exploitation of my body, mind and soul.

As I heal I confront these messages again and again. I am angry that these thoughts stay with me. I am enraged that I was tricked into believing I would want to exploit myself. I feel betrayed and victimized.

I know

~ I did not want to be abused.

~ I did not ask to be abused.

~ I would NOT want to wound my body and soul in such a way.

On a SEPARATE piece of paper I write two messages from the perpetrator. I rip up and throw away the perpetrators messages.

This reminds me that I am now in charge of my life.

In my workbook I create new messages for myself.

For example:

I am learning to like my body, I did not want my body harmed.

I find my strength as I heal and stand my ground.

expression

7 Accountability

Standing My Ground - 2

To remind myself

I am innocent,

I did not cause the abuse,

I am not responsible for the abuse,

I write myself a letter.

Dear (my name),

This letter is to remind me I am not guilty. (Abuser's name) abused me. S/he did (description of one part of the abuse) to me.

S/he is responsible for the abuse. I am not. I am innocent!!!

As I write I remember that I did not cause the abuse. I may call my support people when I have completed this exercise.

expression

112

Standing My Ground - 3

Gradually I start to trust what I am learning.

I am not guilty.

I did not cause the abuse.

I am NOT responsible for the abuse.

I do deserve to heal.

On a SEPARATE piece of paper I create an image of myself when I believe that I am responsible for the abuse. On this image I write words and phrases that keep me thinking that I caused the abuse.

In my workbook I create a second image of myself freed from the belief that I caused the abuse. I write words and phrases that free me from the crippling belief that I caused the abuse.

I compare the two images. I note anything that seems important in my workbook. When I am ready, and if I want to, I throw away the first image.

expression

Standing My Ground - Spiritual Expression

I know the pain of the abuse, the isolation and the belief that I am responsible for the abuse. When others tell me I am not the cause of the abuse I feel hopeful.

Sometimes the feeling of hope brings fear.

Sometimes feeling hopeful is freeing and exciting.

How do I feel when another survivor or helping professional says, "You did not ask for that abuse!"?

How do I feel when there is hope for healing?

I may
~ feel conflicted, frightened or confused.

~ not want the offer of hope from others.

~ feel excited and feel a sense of relief.

~ feel a combination of all these emotions and more.

I write about or create an image of myself when I feel hopeful about my healing and my life.

spiritual expression

Support and Community

> "I tried to get
> through the pain
> by myself—I
> thought it was too
> much to ask my
> friends to share.
> Finding that they
> were there for me
> and that they
> supported the
> person I was
> becoming, was a
> gift beyond belief."
>
> *Survivor*

8

8 *Support and Community*

Giving Myself A Gift

The greatest gift I can give myself today is
the knowledge that I am not alone.

When the abuse occurred
   ~ I was left alone to weep.
   ~ I was alone in the dark.
   ~ no one listened.
   ~ I was terrified.
   ~ I felt alone, isolated, sad and hurt.

Today I am beginning to realize that
   ~ others are available.
   ~ my healing can happen with others
      as witness to me.
   ~ I am not alone.

reading

116

Giving Myself A Gift - 1

As the spiral of healing from abuse continues
I know that I can

~ confront each new fear.

~ write about my fears.

~ share my fears.

~ speak my truth.

In doing these things, I change my habits of
isolation. I move forward in my life and
recovery.

I list my fears about sharing my recovery, my
memories and my story with others.

expression

Giving Myself A Gift - 2

When I choose to

  be with a friend,
  call a friend,
  call a helpline,
  call another survivor,
  attend a support meeting,

I give myself a gift.

When I give to myself

~ I know I am not alone.

~ I feel connected.

~ I get safe with my circle of support.

I write about how I feel when I connect with
    another.

or -

I create an image of my support circle.

expression

Giving Myself A Gift - 3

Part of healing is finding a person or people
I can trust with my story.

As I trust others I give myself a gift. I write
about or create an image of myself
receiving support from others.

expression

8 *Support and Community*

Giving Myself A Gift -
Spiritual Expression

When I connect with the world of nature around me, I am reminded of something greater than myself.

I give myself the gift of beauty, wonder, awe and delight.

On a walk I discover that the trees, birds or the sky remind me that I am not alone.

I create an image of how the natural world reminds me that I am not alone.

or -

I find a favorite photograph or nature postcard to remind myself I am not alone.

I find some way to keep my image visible to me.

This reminds me to
~ connect with nature each day.

~ reach for a connection with something greater than myself.

expression

120

Out Of Isolation

When the abuse happened,
I was alone, isolated from others.

Sometimes
~ I want to stay alone.
~ I do not trust others.
~ I do not want others to witness my
   pain.
~ I am afraid to ask others into my life.
~ I believe that others do not want to
   be with me.

I want people in my life who will:
LAUGH WITH ME
        HOLD ME
                DREAM WITH ME

CARE FOR ME
        PLAY WITH ME
                ENCOURAGE ME

LISTEN TO ME
        GIVE ME FEEDBACK
                TALK TO ME

SHARE WITH ME
        CREATE WITH ME
                BE WITH ME
I want a support community in my life.

I can learn to trust others,
        ~ be with others,
        ~ allow others to witness my loss,
        ~ and witness the healing of others.

I can learn that
        ~ others want to be with me,
        ~ that I have something to offer,
        ~ and that I deserve a support network.

reading

121

8 Support and Community

Out Of Isolation - 1

On whom do I count for support? Why?

Where in my community can I find a support system?

Where are helpline numbers so I can use a phone support system?

Do I want to use 12 Step programs as part of my support community? Have I? How has this felt to me?

What prevents me from creating a support network?

How do I stop myself?

What do I say to myself?

Writing down my thoughts in response to one or more of these questions aids me in the creation of my support network.

expression

Out Of Isolation - 2

Reaching out to others empowers me. I discover how to do a reality check. I ask for feedback on my story, my growth, my healing process.

I can ask other survivors
   Have you ever felt this way?
   How do I sound?
   Am I making sense?

I might get perspective from
   other survivors,
   a friend,
   a professional who is trained to work with
survivors of sexual abuse.

I respond to these questions:
~ Who does provide feedback for me as I heal?
~ Do I need others to provide additional feedback?
~ Is the feedback I am getting helpful to me?
~ Is my gut feeling an additional way I give myself feedback?

expression

8 *Support and Community*

Out Of Isolation - 3

Building a community of support and friendship is a long-term goal and an important part of my healing process.

In the time I take for myself today I list what qualities I would like to have in my friendships and the people in my support community.

expression

Out Of Isolation - Spiritual Expression

I am building a network of support in my life. Often, as a survivor of abuse, I am not trustful of others. Recovery means building trust and creating a support network. Connecting with others is critical to my healing.

I make an effort each day to speak to a friend or support person. When I do this I am reminded that I deserve support.

I create an image of myself surrounded by my support community.

I write about the feelings the image evokes.

spiritual expression

Families

Talking with family members who are in denial about the sexual abuse is difficult and painful.

> ~ Some family members
>   do not believe me,
>   resist what I say,
>   do not want to talk to me.

Sometimes my conversations with family
     members go awry.

I ask myself
> ~ what is family?
> ~ what does family mean to me?
> ~ how do I wish to be with my family?

As I grow my family relationships will
     probably change.
I discover that I can decide
> ~ what I want from my family.
> ~ what I would like from others.
> ~ what family and extended family
>   means to me.
> ~ what I want from those whom I call
>   family.

I also discover
> ~ family has numerous meanings.
> ~ I am the designer of my healing
>   family.
> ~ I can stretch my definition of family.

reading

126

Families - 1

Today I write down words and images I associate with the word family. These may be words from my family of origin, my family now, friends' families or my ideal family.

I circle the words that describe my family of origin.

I respond in writing or with an image to two or more of these questions:

~ How do I feel about my list?

~ What, if anything, surprises me about my words or images?

~ What feels "family-like" about the family I grew up in?

~ What do I like about my family?

~ What displeases me about my family?

~ What do I like now that I did not like as a child?

~ Are there things I did not like as a child and I do not like now?

expression

8 *Support and Community*

Families - 2

What was it like to grow up in my family of origin?

Today I write a letter from the child-me to the adult-me. I let the child describe the family, as the child inside experienced it. I let the child-me state her/his needs at the close of the letter.

Dear_____(fill in your name):

This is _____(inner child's name)...

I may choose to share this letter with someone from my support system.

expression

Families - 3

As I grow I become clear about what I want in a family and what family means to me.

What is my definition of a healing family?

How would I feel in this family?

Where can I go today to start to create this family?

Friends? A support group? Current family members?

I write or create an image of my vision of a healing family.

expression

Families - Spiritual Expression

Sexual abuse and exploitation are not limited by city, state or country boundaries. We are members of a global community.

Today I ask myself how I can contribute to the well-being of other survivors?

When I am ready, I can link up with a local or national helpline. I can contribute to the work that local, national and international organizations are doing. I can contribute, time, money, resources or ideas.

As I heal I join forces with others, from all over the world, who as survivors, are growing beyond abuse. How can I link up with my global family? I write down specific ideas in my workbook.

spiritual expression

Sexuality

> "I am a woman. I am a sexual woman. Now I choose who and when and why and how I express my sexuality. This I know—all expression will be with heart and respect."
>
> *Survivor*

9

My Sexuality Has Been Affected

I feel ignorant about my sexuality. I was deeply affected by the abuse. I feel shame. I feel invaded and ignored. I feel depleted and wounded beyond rational belief.

The most private areas of my life have been
    invaded, turned upside down.
I have developed numerous coping skills to
    deal with my feelings of shame, ignorance,
    fear and terror.

Sometimes
    ~ I pretend I am confident about my
        sexuality.
    ~ I ignore my sexual needs or wants.
    ~ I act out sexually.
    ~ I "numb out" areas of my body.
    ~ I don't allow myself to have sexual
        feelings.

I do not always know how I want to express
    myself sexually.
I do not always want to express myself
    sexually.
I cannot express myself sexually.

I have a rush of sexual energy, feelings,
    images or thoughts.
I do not know how to cope.
With the aid of others I can heal. I can
    reclaim my sexuality!

reading

My Sexuality Has Been
Affected - 1

Healing sexually is tough but not impossible. I feel crippled because of the sexual abuse and I wonder if others feel this way. I need to talk with other survivors and find out what effects they have experienced.

Hearing how others have been affected validates my own experience.

I may hear echoes of how I feel when I listen to others. Including others in my recovery strengthens my commitment to my own healing.

How has my sexuality been affected by the abuse? I write my response to this question.

expression

133

9 *Sexuality*

My Sexuality Has Been Affected - 2

Sometimes memories intrude when I am engaged in sexual expression. In response I may numb out or turn off.

Sometimes I may shut down all sexual feelings for an extended period of time.

What do I say to myself when memories intrude?

Do I say
~ I am bad?
~ I should not be dealing with this any longer?
~ I ought to be healed?

What could I say when memories intrude?

I might say
~ I do not have to feel sexual all the time.
~ It is o.k. for me to shut down.
~ I need to do that sometimes.

Today I write down what I have said to myself and what I would like to say to myself when memories intrude.

expression

134

My Sexuality Has Been Affected - 3

When memories intrude during sexual expression how would I like to be comforted?

Though I may not be ready to share these thoughts with my partner, I write down what I would like my partner to say to me when memories intrude during sexual expression.

or -

I create an image of myself free from sexually intrusive memories.

expression

9 *Sexuality*

My Sexuality Has Been Affected - Spiritual Expression

During my time today I create two images:

~ an image of myself with a sexual wound.

and-

~ an image of myself healing my sexual wound.

What do I learn from these two images?

~ How are they the same?

~ How are they different?

spiritual
expression

136

Sexual Thoughts And Feelings Are Natural

I am learning to enjoy sexual thoughts and feelings again. This is a big step in my recovery from sexual abuse. For a long time I believed that I was responsible for what occurred when I was abused.

I am learning
- ~ that I was not responsible.
- ~ that I may be confused because I may have had sexual feelings when I was abused.
- ~ that if I was sexually aroused during the abuse I am not bad.
- ~ sexual feelings are a natural part of living.

In my healing
- ~ I am beginning to know myself as a person with sexual and sensual feelings.
- ~ I am learning how I want to express those feelings.
- ~ I like learning that sexual responses and feelings are natural.

These thoughts free me to continue my recovery.

reading

137

9 *Sexuality*

Sexual Thoughts And Feelings Are Natural - 1

As I learn about the effects of sexual abuse I discover that some of my ideas about intimacy are confused and somewhat limited.

I am learning

~ that intimacy does not always mean expressing myself sexually.

~ that I have choices about how and with whom I am sexual.

~ that I have sexual feelings and they are okay (or great!).

Taking time for myself I write down some of my beliefs about sexuality.

For example:

I thought the only way to love someone was to be sexual.

I also write down what I am discovering and learning about sexuality.

For example:

I decide when I want to be sexual.

I can say no when I do not want to be sexual.

I can follow through with my decisions.

expression

Sexual Thoughts And Feelings Are Natural - 2

As a result of the abuse I find that sometimes I am left with a legacy of confused sexual thoughts and feelings about sexuality and my sexual feelings.

I sometimes struggle with myself when I remember that I may have had sexual feelings while I was being abused. This horrifies me and I feel angry and confused.

As I talk with helping professionals and other survivors I discover

~ that others also remember having sexual feelings during the abuse.

~ that my body has sexual responses and responded sexually to the abuse.

~ that this does not mean I liked the abuse, nor does it mean I wanted the abuse to happen.

Recovering, I learn that for my body to respond to sexual stimulation was natural.

Today I write down any questions I may have about any sexual feelngs I had during the abuse.

or-

I write down any questions I have about my sexuality.

expression

9 *Sexuality*

Sexual Thoughts And Feelings Are Natural - 3

I am committed to healing.

I am committed to my sexual expression.

I ask myself what coping skills I have developed to deal with the effects of the abuse on my sexual expression.

> Do I ignore my needs and wants?
>   Am I silent?
> Do I act out? Act aggressively?
> Do I hurt others or myself?

What do I need from others to aid me in my healing?

I write down coping skills I have developed to deal with the abuse.

or -

I create an image of myself coping with the abuse.

I may share these thoughts or my image with another.

expression

Sexual Thoughts And Feelings Are Natural - Spiritual Expression

*T*oday I celebrate my sexuality.

I remember that sexuality includes laughter, play, creativity, touching and holding.

I remind myself that sexual thoughts, feelings and ideas are a lovely and natural part of me.

Today I celebrate my sexuality. I name areas of my body that I like to touch, or have touched.

or -

I write about ways I might remind myself that sexual thoughts and feelings are natural.

spiritual expression

Sexual Pleasure

Sometimes I think that
~ I caused the abuse.
~ because I was not strong enough I caused the abuse.
~ if I caused the abuse, I do not deserve pleasure.
~ I do not deserve a sexually loving relationship.

Sometimes
~ I can not speak of the abuse.
~ I am afraid that speaking will ruin everything.
~ I think I do not deserve to speak.
~ I push my sexual needs and wants down.
~ I do not feel them.
~ telling my significant other that I have sexual pleasures and desires is frightening.

Deep inside I wonder if I deserve sexual pleasure.
~ I do not say I need to be held, I want to be kissed.
~ I do not always know what I want!!

Sometimes
~ I start to think I can change this.
~ I start to think I want to change these thoughts and feelings.
~ I feel strong enough to start to change.

Sometimes
~ I believe that I deserve sexual pleasure!
~ I am beginning to know I deserve sexual pleasure!

r e a d i n g

Sexual Pleasure - 1

I do deserve sexual pleasure.

What pleasures me?

~ Exercising?

~ Warmed sheets?

~ Sunlight on my body?

~ Touching? Holding? Stroking? Kissing?
  Fondling?

What pleasures me?

I write down my pleasures. I create an image
  of what feels pleasurable to me. I fantasize
  in a non-harmful way about what
  pleasures me.

I deserve sexual pleasure.

expression

9 *Sexuality*

Sexual Pleasure - 2

What would I like to tell myself about sexual pleasure?

Today I write myself a letter. I write my feelings and thoughts about sexual pleasure. I write about how the abuse affected my thoughts about my sexual pleasure.

or -

I write affirmations about sexual pleasure for myself.

expression

Sexual Pleasure - 3

I deserve to talk about myself and my sexuality. I deserve to celebrate. I deserve a sexual relationship, sexual pleasure.

I am not guilty, stupid, bad or shameful. I did not cause the abuse. What do I say to myself about my sexuality, the abuse, sexual relationships?

Do I say

~ I could have protected myself.

~ I could have stopped the abuse. I should have left.

~ I had sexual feelings, therefore I asked to be abused.

In my workbook I write what I say to myself.

Could I say

~ I am acquiring tools to protect myself now.

~ I could not have stopped the abuse and I am learning what abuse is.

~ I have sexual feelings, BUT I did not ask for the abuse, I did not deserve the abuse.

In my workbook I write what I could say to myself.

expression

9 *Sexuality*

Sexual Pleasure - Spiritual Expression

*E*ach day the earth celebrates. She gives abundantly.

Rain, grass, trees, flowers, sunlight and moonlight.

We are the beneficiaries of this abundant nature. Sexual expression is an abundant giving, a time of play, laughter and celebration. Alone, or with another, we are sexual beings.

Today I celebrate my sexuality by,

~ sitting in the sun, sitting in a sauna,

~ taking a nap on clean sheets.

Today I rediscover and celebrate my sexuality. I remind myself that the very earth celebrates and gives in an abundant way.

I will do one or more things to celebrate my sexuality. (I might be held by another, walk in nature, paint a picture).

or -

I write about or create an image of how the earth celebrates her sexuality.

spiritual
expression

Celebration

*"To celebrate is to
recognize grace and
to honor recovery.
It is the expression
of a free spirit.
Now I am free."*

Survivor

10

10 Celebration

A Celebration Of My Healing

Sharing my story with safe people
~ I learn to believe my story.
~ I learn to accept feedback, support.
~ I receive information, ideas,
thoughts.

Telling my story to others brings me gifts.
~ I cry with others.
~ I laugh with others.
~ I discover commonalities between us.
~ I discover that I am not alone.
~ I feel welcomed and witnessed.
These are gifts.

Listening to others
~ I gain acceptance of myself.
~ I learn to accept others.
~ I find companions.
~ I learn to speak without fear.
~ I find tears, humor, laughter, grief,
sorrow and healing.

Speaking my story,
listening to others,
is a celebration of healing.
A celebration of my song.

reading

148

10 Celebration

A Celebration Of My Healing - 1

I create an image of myself sharing my story with others. I may draw, sculpt, paint or create a collage.

or -

I reflect and write about these questions:

~ What might I receive as I share my story?

~ What might I contribute to others as I share?

~ How does this feel to me to share my story?

expression

10 *Celebration*

A Celebration Of My Healing - 2

How do I feel when someone listens to me?

What happens inside me when someone really listens?

Whom do I talk with, who hears me?

How does telling my story, and being heard, effect my healing?

Today I respond to one or more of these questions in writing or by creating an image.

expression

A Celebration Of My Healing - 3

What happens to me when I really listen to someone else?

How do I feel?

What pleases me most when I listen to another?

How does hearing the story of another survivor help me?

What gifts do I give? What gifts do I receive?

I respond to the questions that appeal most to me.

or -

If none of these questions fit my life I write about or create an image of myself listening to others.

expression

10 Celebration

A Celebration Of My Healing -
Spiritual Expression

*T*oday I celebrate.

I celebrate that I listen to others!

I celebrate that I am heard!

I celebrate breaking the silence!

I celebrate speaking my truth!

I may dance, sing, go for a walk, buy fresh cut
flowers, call a friend. I may paint a picture
of myself with others. I may go out to
dinner with a friend.

Today I celebrate the spirit of freedom that
comes from:

~ speaking with others.

~ listening to others.

I note in my workbook how I celebrated and
how I felt as I celebrated.

*spiritual
expression*

I Reclaim My Hidden Dreams

While I was being sexually abused, as a way
to stay safe, I stopped myself from dreaming.

As a result of the abuse
   ~ I thought the future would always be
     as painful as the present.
   ~ I stopped creating a future for me.

Sometimes
   ~ I still stop my dreams about healthy
     friendships, fulfilling work, loves,
     home and future.
   ~ I stop myself from dreaming about
     the small everyday things like
     gardening, walking, enjoying the
     beauty of the lakes, a sunset or the
     quiet of the early morning.

As I heal
   ~ I realize that I have always had
     dreams.
   ~ I understand my dreams do not have
     to stay hidden.
   ~ I retrieve old dreams and create new
     dreams.
   ~ I remember the abuse, I also
     remember the dreams.
   ~ I dream again.

I welcome and embrace my dreams, my
   dreaming!
I reclaim my hidden dreams!.

reading

I Reclaim My Hidden Dreams - 1

In the course of the abuse my boundaries were invaded over and over. My focus became narrowed and restricted.

Before my recovery began

~ I was unaware of my dreams.

~ I was more aware of the dreams of others.

~ It seemed easier to give up my dreams and enter into the dreams of others.

Part of my recovery

~ is reclaiming my dreams.

~ is listening to myself so I know and respond to my dreams.

I list my dreams.

I look back in my memory to bring forward dreams I had before the abuse.

I write these down.

I begin to reclaim my hidden dreams.

expression

I Reclaim My Hidden Dreams - 2

Dreaming is a creative and energizing force in my life.

I deserve to dream my future exactly the way I want it to be.

~ I want to have a habit of dreaming.

~ I want to reclaim my hidden dreams.

I write down what dreams I have for myself.

For example:

~ I deserve to have one more friend in six months.

expression

10 Celebration

I Reclaim My Hidden Dreams - 3

Today I close my eyes and allow the child within to speak to me about forgotten or put away dreams. Maybe it was a walk in a special woods, a certain book I wanted to read or a person I wanted to meet. Maybe my dream was a trip to India or China, maybe my dream was to learn to garden or grow flowers.

Reclaiming this childhood dream, I celebrate myself again. I want to affirm that the child within has every right to dream anything!

I ask the child what s/he wants most, what is her/his dream?

I create an image of a childhood dream. I write down how I can make that dream come true.

expression

I Reclaim My Hidden Dreams
- Spiritual Expression

Dreaming is celebration.

Today, as I focus on celebration,

~ I think of a dream I have had that I have fulfilled.

~ I write this dream down.

~ I create ideas of how to celebrate this dream.

~ I celebrate my accomplishment and write down how I celebrate.

Accomplishing a dream is a reason to celebrate. I celebrate my dreams.

spiritual expression

10 Celebration

Laughing, I heal

I love to laugh!

I love to play!

I love

~ laughter bubbling up inside of me.
~ the sun moving on the grass.
~ giggling with friends.
~ belly laughing with those I love.

I grin when I think of my small, inner person
and I laugh
~ when I see children playing,
~ when I slide and swing,
~ when I dance until I am breathless.
~ when I watch my pet playing.

I share
~ laughter,
~ humor,
~ play,
with my friends and myself.
I am freer, happier, more playful.

reading

158

Laughing, I heal - 1

What gets in the way when I play?

How do I feel about playing?

Is life supposed to be serious all the time?

What happens when I laugh with friends?

How do I treat myself when I am not in a laughing mood?

How do I treat myself when I want to laugh and giggle?

I write or create an image of what prevents me from playing. I also create an image of myself playing. What do the two images tell me?

expression

Laughing, I Heal - 2

I would like to laugh one time today.

~ I may ask someone to tell me a corny joke.

~ I may watch a funny movie.

~ I may think of something very funny that has happened in my life.

I would like to laugh one time today. I write about what makes me laugh? Do I like to laugh? With whom do I laugh?

expression

Laughing, I Heal - 3

*T*oday I give myself 15 minutes of playtime.

I may laugh,

play on a swing set,

go roller skating,

play with a balloon,

blow bubbles, or doodle.

Or I may choose to imagine sharing funny stories with friends as my playtime.

I write down

~ how I play.

~ how I felt as I played.

~ what happened when I had playtime.

~ what happens for me when I claim my laughter, joy and playfulness?

expression

10 Celebration

Laughing, I Heal - Spiritual Expression

Playing and celebrating is a way to go beyond ourselves, to experience others, to experience our own joy and delight in the world.

I create an image of myself laughing and playing with my friends.

or -

What happens inside me as I think about creating images of laughing and playing? How do I feel?

spiritual expression

162

Closing Thoughts

To the survivors of sexual exploitation and childhood sexual abuse: May you find hope in knowing, that as survivors, we can always dig a little deeper through the rubble of sexual abuse and find the absolute truth about our innate goodness.

Laurel Lewis

My hope is that all persons who have survived abuse grow to learn of the intrinsic and lovely beauty of their nature.

Signe L. Nestingen

Resources

Growing Beyond Abuse is a catalyst for stretching yourself toward new ideas, thoughts, feelings and beliefs. We have included the following resources to encourage you to stretch yourself as you grow and heal.

Comparisons- Incestuous Family Systems and Sexual Exploitation

INCEST	EXPLOITATION
The well-being of the child is the responsibility of the family or kinship circle. When a child is sexually abused the well-being of the child is ignored and trust is violated.	A therapist who exploits a client does not have the well being of the client in mind. The trust of the client is violated.
In incestuous families the authority and power of the adults are used to abuse the children. Somtimes older children learn to abuse others in the kinship circle.	In a therapeutic relationship the therapist is in a position of authority and power. In an exploitative situation that power is used to seduce and harm the client.
The incestuous kinship circle will not allow new information to flow into it, therefore all needs must be satisfied within that circle. The dependent child learns to live in an abusive and closed system.	Exploitative systems are closed systems. Increased dependency on the therapist is cultivated. For someone from an abusive background this may feel familiar and enticing.
The child is robbed of an opportunity to develop a value system and sense of self. Values a child may have developed arc disregarded.	The values of the client are disregarded and the client's self concept may be threatened or damaged.
In incestuous systems secrets are mandated.	Secret keeping is a cornerstone in an exploitative relationship.
The abused child/children are made to feel special. In this way their needs are disregarded and the seduction gains momentum.	A therapist may establish a special relationship with a client, (e.g. verbally telling the client s/he is special, inviting the client to social or family functions). This is part of the seduction.
In incestuous systems, the child's need to grow, develop and emancipate is prohibited. This includes the physical, sexual, mental, emotional and spiritual developmental needs of the child.	The emotional, mental, sexual and spiritual help that the client so desparately needs are often lost in the rubble of exploitation. The client may lose several years which are irretrievable.
The child's basic need for safety is ignored; this may result in physical injury and symptomology.	A client may experience physical repercussions due to the stress of exploitation.
Boundaries are violated within the incest systems, parent - child roles are distorted.	As the boundaries are violated, the needs of the therapist take precedent and the clients' needs are disregarded.
The child is under the care of the adult in all cases. This makes the child vulnerable to the adult.	The therapist often becomes a parental figure due to transference. This phenomenon makes the client particularly vulnerable.

Growing Beyond Abuse   © 1990, Nestingen and Lewis

Wheel of Options for Victims of Sexual Exploitation

Report to County or State Authorities

Do Nothing

Notify Church Hierarchy or Agency Director

Civil Suit for Damages

Complaint to Ethics Comm. of Professional Association

Licensure Complaint

Compensation From Victim's Fund

The Client

Write or Call Ex-counselor

Confrontation/ Processing Session

Private Compensation For Damages

Individual or Group Therapy for Client

Criminal Complaint

"This 'Wheel' does not imply random selection, rather it suggests that there is no linear hierarchy, and that a combination of choices may be appropriate." J. Milgrom

Wheel of Options and quote reprinted from *Psychotherapists' Sexual Involvement with Clients: Intervention and Prevention.* © 1989 Schoener, Milgrom, Gonsiorek, Luepker and Conroe.

Sexual Exploitation is an isolating, degrading and divisive experience. As you heal we strongly recommend that you connect with others. You can do this by finding an advocate, talking with other survivors, forming support groups and joining existing support or therapy groups.

Connecting with others you may find that you are ready to pursue legal options, talk with licensing agencies or file a complaint.*

Although it is not always necessary, if you wish to work with a therapist we urge you to find a qualified, competent and helpful therapist. On the next page we provide some guidelines for choosing a competent therapist.

Signe L. Nestingen, M.A.

*For information about these issues you can call the helpline numbers listed in the back of this book.

There are several things you can do as you look for a qualified and competent therapist with whom to work. We have included this list to give you some ideas about how to find a therapist*.

1. For names and numbers of therapists in your area ask local helplines or organizations who works with survivors of exploitation and abuse.

2. Ask other survivors for the names and numbers of therapists.

3. Has the therapist worked with survivors of sexual exploitation and/or childhood sexual abuse? For how long?

4. How long has the therapist been practicing in this state? Other states? Which other states?

5. Ask the person with whom you wish to work if s/he is licensed. By which licensing board? (They might be a licensed social worker, psychiatrist, psychologist, etc.). Is s/he a member of any professional organizations? Which ones?

6. Ask to <u>see</u> the ethical guidelines for any licensing or professional organizations of which the therapist is a member.

7. Ask for the phone numbers of the local boards with which the therapist is licensed. Call the licensing boards and ask if there has ever been a complaint filed about the therapist with whom you wish to work.

8. Does the therapist seek consultation or supervision on a regular or as needed basis? In other words, is this therapist willing to ask for help as necessary?

9. Are there other professionals who would be willing to provide recommendations? Who? What are their names and numbers?

10. If you wish to, go for an initial interview session with the therapist. (Expect to pay for the session). See how it feels, ask questions and look around. Are you comfortable in this office? Write down your thoughts and talk with others about your visit.

11. Ask the therapist about the costs, therapy goals, and the therapeutic contract. Do these things make sense? Are they in line with other therapists in the community?

12. Pay close attention to your own insides, if things do not feel right, talk about it with other survivors or call a helpline with professionals on staff.

*The term therapist includes psychotherapists, pastoral counselors, physicians, nurses, psychiatrists, social workers, psychologists, chemical dependency counselors and other mental health professionals.

<u>*Growing Beyond Abuse*</u>   © 1990, Nestingen and Lewis

Walk-In-Counseling Center
2421 Chicago Avenue South
Minneapolis, MN 55404
(612) 870-0565

IMPACT
(In Motion - People Abused in
Counseling and Therapy)
323 South Pearl Street
Denver, CO 80209
(303) 979-8073

BASTA - Boston Association to
Stop Therapy Abuse
528 Franklin Street
Cambridge, MA 02139
(617) 661-4667

Marie Fortune
1914 N. 34th Street
Suite #105
Seattle, WA 98103
(206) 634-1906

Stop ABC (Abuse By Counselors)
Box 68292
Seattle, WA 98168
(206) 243-2723
(contact Shirley Siegel)

TELL (Therapy Exploitation Link
Line)
P.O. Box 115
Waban, MA 02168
(617) 964-TELL

AACEP - Association Against Client
Exploitation by Professionals
P.O. Box 533
Havertown, PA 19803
(215) 449-6663

Forbidden Zone Recovery
1580 Valencia St.
Suite 601
San Francisco, CA 94110
(415) 572-0571
(408) 978-1597

Forbidden Zone Recovery
1101 SW Washington
Suite 173
Portland OR 97205
(503) 241-6032
(please include self-addressed
envelope)

CCRT - California Consumer's for
Responsible Therapy
P.O. Box 2194
Garden Grove, CA 92642-2194

Incest Resources, Inc.
46 Pleasant Street
Cambridge, MA 02139
(Please write for information)

Incest Survivors Resource
Network International
P.O.Box 7375
Los Cruces, NM 88006-7375
(education resource for organizations)

W.I.N.G.S.
Women Incest - Needing Group
Support
Foundation, Inc.
(303) 238-8660
Denver, Co

Parents United International
Adults Molested as Children United
(AMACU)
P.O.Box 952
San Jose, CA 95108
(408) 453-7616

C. Henry Kempe Center
1205 Oneida Street
Denver, CO 80220
(303) 321-3963

Childhelp USA
1345 El. Centro Avenue
P.O. Box 630
Hollywood, CA 90028
(213) 465-4016
Hotline # (800) 4ACHILD

National Office of Childhelp USA
6463 Independence Avenue
Woodland Hills, CA 91367
(818) 347-7280

National Committee for the
Prevention of Child Abuse
332 South Michigan Avenue
Suite 950
Chicago, IL 60604
(312) 663-3520
(Provides free catalogue of sources)

VOICES In Action, Inc.
P.O. Box 148309
Chicago, IL 60614
(312) 327-1500
(phone calls are returned collect)

Looking Up
P.O. Box K
Augusta, ME 04332-0470

NEWSLETTERS

Survivior Network
P.O. Box 80058
Albuquerque, NM 87198

PLEA
356 W. Zia Rd.
Santa Fe, NM 87505

Incest Survivor Information
Exchange
P.O. Box 3399
New Haven, CT 06515

Resource Books for Survivors and Professionals

Childhood Sexual Abuse

Bryant, Marcella. *Ancient Child, Poetry about Incest.* Texas: Plain View Press, 1989.

Goodwin, Jean M. *Incest Victims and Their Families.* Chicago: Year Book Medical, 1989.

Lew, Mike. *Victims No Longer: Men Recovering from Incest and Other Child Sexual Abuse.* New York: Nevraumont Publishing, 1988.

Kane, Evangeline. *Recovering From Incest. Imagination and the Healing Process.* Boston: Sigo Press, 1989

Maltz, Wendy and Beverly Holman. *Incest and Sexuality: A Guide to Understanding and Healing.* Lexington: Lexington Press, 1987.

Randall, Margaret. *This is about Incest.* Ithaca: Firebrand Books, 1987.

Wisechild, Louise. *The Obsidian Mirror,* Seattle: Seal Press, 1988.

Bear, Euan and Peter Dimmock. *Adults Molested as Children: A Survivors Manual for Women and Men.* Vermont: Safer Society Press, 1988.

Crewdson, John. *By Silence Betrayed, Sexual Abuse of Children in America.* New York: Harper and Row, 1988.

Bass, Ellen and Laura Davis. *The Courage to Heal - A Guide for Woman Survivors of Child Sexual Abuse.* NewYork: Harper & Row,1988.

Janssen, Martha. *Silent Scream. I am a Victim of Incest.* Philadelphia: Fortress Press, 1983.

Courtois, Christine. *Healing the Incest Wound.* New York: Norton, 1988.

Herman, Judith Lewis. *Father-Daughter Incest.* Cambridge: Harvard University, 1981.

Sexual Exploitation

Rutter, Peter. *Sex in the Forbidden Zone.* Los Angeles: Tarcher, 1989.

Fortune, Marie. *Is Nothing Sacred.* San Francisco: Harper & Row, 1989.

Bates, Carolyn M. and Annette M. Brodskey. *Sex in the Therapy Hour.* New York: Guilford Press, 1989.

Gabbard M.D., Glen O. *Sexual Exploitation in Professional Relationships.* USA: American Psychiatric Press, 1989.

Schoener, Milgrom, Gonsiorek, Luepker, Conroe. *Psychotherapists' Sexual Involvement with Clients: Intervention and Prevention.* Minneapolis: Walk-In Counseling Center, 1989.
(Call or write for order information: 2421 Chicago Ave. S. Minneapolis, MN 55404 (612) 870-0565.)

Sanderson, Barbara E. (Ed.). *It's Never OK: A Handbook for Professionals on Sexual Exploitation by Counselors and Therapists,* St. Paul: Minnesota Department of Corrections, 1989.
(Call or write for or information:
MN Program for Victims of Sexual Assult.
MN Dept. of Corrections 300 Bigelow Bldg.
450 N. Syndicate Street, St. Paul, MN 55104
(612) 642-0256)

Miller, Alice. *Thought Shalt Not be Aware.* New York: Farrar Straus Giroux, 1984.

Miller, Alice. *For Your Own Good, Hidden Cruelties in Childhood.* New York: Farrar Straus Giroux, 1983.

White, William. *Incest in the Organization Family: The Ecology of Burnout in Closed Systems.* Illinois: Lighthouse Training Institute, 1986.
(Call or write for information: 702 W. Chestnut, Bloomington, Illinois 61701, (309) 827-6026).

Freeman, Lucy and Julie Roy. *Betrayal.* New York: Stein and Day, 1976.

Plasil, Ellen. *Therapist:* New York: St. Martin Press, 1985.

Walker, Evelyn and T.D. Young. *A Killing Cure.* New York: Henry Holt and Co., 1986.

Olsen Jack: *Doc-The Rape of the Town of Lovell.* New York: Ateneum 1989.

Striano, Judi. *Can Therapists Hurt You?* Santa Barbara: Professional Press.

Striano, Judi. *How to Find A Good Psychotherapist; A Consumer Guide.* Santa Barbara: Professional Press.

Chester, Pellauer, Boyajian, *Sexual Assult and Abuse; A Handbook for Clergy and Religious Professionals.* San Francisco: Harper and Row, 1987.

Burgess, Ann, and Carol Hartman. *Sexual Exploitation by Health Professionals.* New York: Praeger Press, 1986.

Sexual Intimacy Between Therapists and Patients. New York: Praeger Press, 1986. (In Libraries).

Resource Books for Survivors and Professionals

Other Books for Healing

McLearran, Alice. *The Mountain that Loved A Bird*. Natick: Picture Book Studio USA, 1985.

Piercy, Marge. *The Moon is Always Female*. New York: Knopf, 1984.

Baylor, Byrd. *I'm In Charge of Celebrations*. New York: MacMillan, 1986.

Hindman, Jan, *A Very Touching Book*. Oregon: AlexAndria Assoc.

Satir, Virginia. Self-Esteem. California: *Celestial Arts*, 1975.

Casey, Karen. *Each Day a New Beginning*. Minnesota: Hazelden, 1982.

Angelou, Maya. *I Know Why the Caged Bird Sings*. New York: Bantam, 1980.

The Boston Women's Health Book Collective. *The New Our Bodies, Ourselves*. New York: Simon and Schuster, 1984.

Walker, Alice. *The Color Purple*. New York: Pocketbooks, 1982.

Order Form

Please send me *GROWING BEYOND ABUSE* at $15.95 each,
which includes sales tax.
(Payable in U.S. currency or equivalent).

Number of Books Ordered _____
(includes $3.00 shipping and handling) x $18.95
         Total Cost $_____
Allow 4-6 weeks for delivery.

Make check or money order
payable to:
Omni Recovery, Inc.

Mail this form with payment to
the following address:

Omni Recovery, Inc.
P.O. Box 50033
Minneapolis, Minnesota 55403

Ship to:

Please Print

_____
Name

_____
Organization

_____
Street Address

_____
City

_____
State

_____
Zipcode

Would you like to be on the Omni Recovery, Inc. mailing list?   Yes? _____

Order Form

Please send me *GROWING BEYOND ABUSE* at $15.95 each,
which includes sales tax.
(Payable in U.S. currency or equivalent).

Number of Books Ordered _____
(includes $3.00 shipping and handling) x $18.95
      Total Cost $_____

Allow 4-6 weeks for delivery.

Make check or money order
payable to:
Omni Recovery, Inc.

Mail this form with payment to
the following address:

Omni Recovery, Inc.
P.O. Box 50033
Minneapolis, Minnesota 55403

Ship to:

Please Print

_____
Name

_____
Organization

_____
Street Address

_____
City

_____
State

_____
Zipcode

Would you like to be on the Omni Recovery, Inc. mailing list?   Yes? _____